D0097727

Marine
Aquariums

Fish Keeping
Made Easy ™

Marine Aquariums

Basic Aquarium Setup and Maintenance

Ray Hunziker

BOWTIE
PRESS®

Irvine, California

Karla Austin, *Business Operations Manager*
Nick Clemente, *Special Consultant*
Jarelle S. Stein, *Editor*
Kendra Strey, *Assistant Editor*
Jill Dupont, *Production*
Alleen Winters, *Design*
Indexed by Kenneth Brace

Cover photograph by Oliver Lucanus/Belowwater.com.
All illustrations are by Laurie O'Keefe.
All photographs are by Ray Hunziker unless otherwise noted.
The additional photographs in this book are by: 6, 19, 27, 33, 34, 45,
53, 61, 62, 92 top, 97, 104 top, 106, 107, 112, 115, 117, 127 bottom, 132, 134: Sally McCrae Kuyper; 17, 29, 32, 52: Derk R. Kuyper;
39: (©2005) JupiterImages and its Licensors;18, 51, 60, 72, 75–77, 80,
81 top, 82, 84, 86, 100, 114 top, 120,121, 133: Scott W. Michael.

Library of Congress Cataloging-in-Publication Data

Hunziker, Raymond E.
  Marine aquariums / by Ray Hunziker.
    p. cm.
  ISBN 1-931993-64-5
  1. Marine aquariums. I. Title.
  SF457.1H86 2005
  639.34'2—dc22

BowTie Press®
A Division of BowTie, Inc.
3 Burroughs
Irvine, California 92618

Printed and bound in Singapore
10 9 8 7 6 5 4 3 2 1

Dedicated to Danny and Katie with love from Uncle Ray.

Contents

Introduction: Is a Marine Aquarium Right for You?

Like many before you, you find yourself enchanted by the beauty of the seas and the glorious colors of the fish and other creatures of the coral reef. Having your own marine aquarium will allow you to enjoy that beauty at home. Before taking the plunge, however, ask yourself: Is a marine aquarium right for me? Do I have the experience and the commitment it will take to make it a success?

Experience. I strongly recommend that you spend some time getting your feet wet with freshwater aquaria—learning the basics of water quality, how to select and maintain filters and other equipment, and how to select fish and mix them to create compatible communities. Once you have that "wet thumb," success with a marine aquarium will be more likely.

➲ The bright colors of marine fish make it easy to understand their appeal. Don't head to the fish store too soon—be sure you first understand the requirements of maintaining your aquarium before making that first purchase.

Commitment. You should be a detail-oriented person who doesn't mind maintenance chores and monitoring. If you're willing to devote a minimal amount of time every day, you may be ready for a marine aquarium. There will also be a financial commitment; there's no denying that it's more expensive than a freshwater aquarium. However, marine aquarium–keeping is still cheaper than a lot of other hobbies. You'll almost certainly spend less than a car collector or electronics nut!

I took the plunge into the marine hobby some years ago, and I hope that my experience will help you create a successful and attractive marine aquarium on your first try. First, we'll lay the groundwork with some of the science that makes a marine aquarium work. Then, we'll look at the nuts and bolts of the operation—the aquarium and the equipment that keeps it running smoothly. Finally, we'll consider a cross section of fish you're likely to see at your local fish store. I won't be shy about using both their common and scientific (Latin) names, and neither should you. At the end of our journey, you'll have the most important tools—knowledge and commitment—to make your dream aquarium into a reality.

A WORD ON CONSERVATION

In our ecologically conscious world, marine aquariums pose some controversy. Be an informed consumer. Let your local fish store know that you want them to buy only from collectors who use responsible methods (such as nets, not drugs), to buy aquacultured species when available, and to stock only creatures that can be kept alive in captivity. Additionally, you can support the efforts of groups—such as the Marine Aquarium Council (www.aquariumcouncil.org)—that seek to educate the hobbyist, the local fish store, and the public about responsible collecting and keeping of reef fish and other organisms.

CHAPTER 1

Seawater and Water Quality

Though many people use the terms saltwater *and* seawater *interchangeably, the distinction between the two is important. Seawater is a complex combination of chemicals with interesting and unusual characteristics. Before you start setting up your tank, it's very important to understand what makes up a balanced aquarium, and the most important element is the water itself. What makes seawater special? Why is it important to simulate it as closely as possible in marine aquariums?*

The major component of seawater is good old H_2O. The various elements and compounds that make seawater different from freshwater are dissolved solids, liquids, and gases. The most important of these are salts, and the most abundant salt in seawater is sodium chloride (NaCl), chemically identical to the salt in the shaker on your dinner table. When dissolved in water, salts break into their component atoms. This process is called dissociation. When salts dissociate, their component atoms carry tiny positive and negative electrical charges and are called ions. Scientists measure the amount of salt in seawater by measuring the amounts of the ions sodium (Na^+) and chlorine (Cl^-), along with smaller amounts of other ions.

In fact, although natural seawater contains more than 70 elements, only 7 ions make up nearly 100 percent (by weight) of all the dissolved solids in a volume of seawater: chlorine (Cl^-, ~55.2 percent), sodium (Na^+, ~30.7 percent), sulfate (SO_4^{2-}, ~7.7 percent) magnesium (Mg^{2+}, ~3.7 percent), calcium (Ca^{2+}, ~1.2 percent), potassium (K^+, ~1.1 percent), and bicarbonate (HCO_3^-, ~0.4 percent). If you add up the numbers in this list, you'll see that they equal exactly 100 percent; however, there is a little bit of rounding error involved. Somewhere in the last 1 percent is everything else, referred to as trace elements.

If you used tests that were sensitive enough, you would find a large number of metals in seawater—even copper, gold, and silver. There are also small amounts of dissolved gases, including all those normally found in the atmosphere, such as nitrogen, oxygen, and carbon dioxide. Some of these trace elements and gases are very important to living creatures. For example, if your aquarium had no dissolved oxygen, or too much carbon dioxide, your fish would suffocate. However, some of the trace elements, especially the metals, are toxic when present in quantities greater than the levels found in natural seawater.

Therefore, when obtaining seawater for marine aquariums, it is very important to consider the source. Unfortunately, it's not as simple as going down to the beach, walking out into the surf, and collecting your own natural seawater. In North America it's becoming increasingly tough to find clean coastal seawater. Inshore estuaries are often polluted with heavy metals, petroleum chemicals from boat traffic, and suspended sediment. Artificial sea salt mixes available at your local fish store offer a safer alternative, providing your aquarium with the major, minor, and trace elements found in natural seawater.

SALINITY AND SPECIFIC GRAVITY

❶ Find artificial sea salt mixes such as this sample at your local fish store.

In the vast majority of the world's oceans, the salinity, defined as total dissolved solids, hovers around 35 parts per thousand (ppt). To look at what this means, the math is easier if we go metric. A liter (a little more than a U.S. quart) is composed of 1,000 milliliters (mL); 1 mL of pure distilled water weighs 1 gram (g); so, 1,000 mL = 1,000 g. If we have 1,000 g of seawater, we know that part of this weight is the salt, not the water. If we know that the salinity of that seawater is 35 ppt, what this is really telling us is that we have 965 g (or 965 parts) of water and 35 g (or 35 parts) of "salt." Because the dissolved solids make seawater heavier than distilled water, 1,000 g of seawater will actually have a volume slightly less than that of a liter of distilled water, although the weight will be the same: 1,000 g.

Related to salinity is specific gravity, a measure of how heavy a water sample is compared with pure water. Most tropical, open-ocean water has a specific gravity of approximately 1.025 to 1.026. Because pure water is assigned the reference value of 1.000, a specific gravity of 1.026 is really telling us that that water sample is 1.026 times denser (heavier) than pure water. (See Tank Monitoring in Chapter 3 for further discussion of salinity and specific gravity.)

ALKALINITY AND PH

The simplest definition of pH is the measurement of how acidic or basic a solution is by determining the level of hydrogen ions. The pH scale ranges from 1.0 to 14.0; a reading of 1.0 is very acidic, a reading of 14.0 is very basic (alkaline), and a reading of 7.0 is neutral—that is, with roughly equal amounts of acidic and alkaline chemicals. Natural seawater is moderately alkaline, ranging between 7.8 and 8.4—usually closer to the upper end of this range.

Just as salts dissociate into charged ions, water itself dissociates a little bit. In a sample of water, some of the H_2O molecules will dissociate into hydrogen (H^+) and hydroxyl (OH^-) ions. Hydrogen ions are acidic; they drive the pH down. Hydroxyl ions are alkaline; they drive the pH up. In pure water these dissociations are balanced, so a sample of distilled water should read just about neutral (7.0) on the pH scale. However, salts and other dissolved chemicals in water tend to disrupt the balance. Dissolved chemicals may, for example, add an excess of hydrogen ions to the water and lower the pH, or they may chemically bind to either the hydrogen or hydroxyl ions and essentially remove the ions from the equation.

Whether water is acidic or alkaline, it tends to resist attempts to change it. This effect is called buffering. As mentioned above, sea-water is alkaline; however, the biological processes that occur in an aquarium mostly tend to produce acids. If we don't deal with this tendency, the pH of a marine aquarium will decrease over time until it becomes life-threateningly acidic for our fish. For example, when fish breathe, they exhale carbon dioxide (CO_2), just like you and me. If the water contains too much CO_2, the CO_2 will combine with water to form carbonic acid and will lower the pH. Additionally, some of the waste products produced by animals are acids. Bacterial decomposition can produce acids, and even the beneficial bacteria in filters produce acids. In the ocean, the acids produced by living organisms are either miniscule or removed by large-scale chemical processes, which don't occur in the aquarium.

The pH range of normal seawater is 7.8—8.4

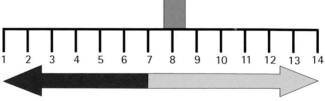

NITROGEN CYCLE

The nitrogen cycle is so called because all of the chemical compounds involved are nitrogenous, meaning that they contain nitrogen (N). You will need to understand how this cycle works and how to monitor it to keep your tank running smoothly and your animals alive.

Fish, like all living organisms, excrete waste products. The primary waste excreted by fish (and by most invertebrates, too) is the nitrogenous compound ammonia (NH_3), usually in the form of the more stable ammonium ion (NH_4^+). Ammonium is very toxic to almost all fish and invertebrates, so we need some method of dealing with it. Fortunately, there are beneficial nitrifying bacteria that grow in your filter, on the grains of sand or gravel on the bottom of your tank, and on just about every other surface in your aquarium. The nitrifying bacteria are aerobic, which means they need oxygen to function—in the same way you need oxygen when you do aerobic exercise. When they have plenty of oxygen, the nitrifying bacteria convert the ammonium into nitrite (NO_2). Nitrite is still toxic, but far less toxic than ammonium. The nitrifying bacteria then take the nitrite and convert it into nitrate (NO_3). Nitrate is far less toxic than either of its predecessors. In fact, most fish are not bothered by it unless the level is very high (though, soft-bodied invertebrates can still be pretty sensitive to it).

A basic understanding of the chemistry of seawater will help you better understand the importance of properly mixing and measuring your marine aquarium water. (See Tank Monitoring in Chapter 3 for more information.)

Nitrogen Cycle

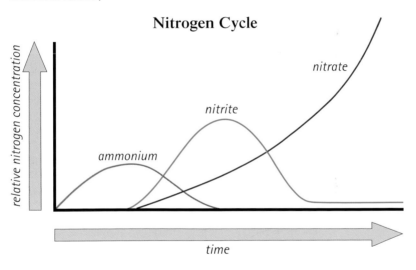

relative nitrogen concentration

nitrate

nitrite

ammonium

time

Setting Up a Marine Aquarium

Since we now understand a little bit more about the unique properties of seawater, we can start to take a look at the basic setup of a marine aquarium, beginning with the various equipment and tools. What type of aquarium should you choose? Where should you put it? How do you make sure it is safely supported? What are your options for bottom coverings and decorations? What accessory devices will you need? Finally, how do you select appropriate fish for the tank you've selected?

AQUARIUM TYPES

Although there are other types of aquariums, there are really only two that are practical for the home hobbyist: glass and acrylic. Most glass aquariums are rectangular, with four flat sides and a bottom held together with silicone cement. They are less expensive than acrylic, but they are also much heavier and more breakable. Acrylic aquariums are relatively lightweight, stronger, optically clearer, more flexible, and more shatter-resistant than glass. Because acrylic is a plastic, it can be molded into a variety of shapes. However, acrylic has some definite disadvantages: it scratches easily, may yellow with age, and is much more expensive than glass. Visit your local fish store for a look at both types of aquarium—preferably assembled and running—so that you can make an informed decision. Most aquarists choose glass, usually for its lower price. Whether you choose acrylic or glass, buy the largest aquarium you can afford; in a larger volume of water, common beginners' errors such as overfeeding are less likely to lead to lethal poisoning. At the very least, you should have more time to correct the error by making a partial water change.

In recent years, aquarium manufacturers have embraced the idea that an aquarium can be more than a glass box that holds water and fish. When the tank, cover, lighting fixtures, and stand are designed with the same trim and finishing, they can make a stunningly attractive piece of furniture that is a tasteful accent to any room. There is nothing wrong with the standard rectangular aquarium from a visual standpoint; but if you want to be creative, there are more tank shape options than ever before, including pentagons (which work well in a corner), octagons, bowfronts, and others. If you're trying to create a design theme for a room, you can be confident there is an aquarium that is perfect for your personal style.

STOCKING CALCULATION

One of the most difficult questions to answer definitively is that of how many fish can be placed in a marine aquarium. You should consider this fundamental question, as it will help you determine the ideal aquarium size and shape for your purposes. Many of you have probably heard the old freshwater aquarist's rule of thumb: "an inch of fish per gallon of water." Unfortunately, territoriality often complicates this equation. In both freshwater and marine tanks, I have seen 2-inch (5-cm) fish that were aggressive enough to claim an entire 20- or 30-gallon (76- or 114-L) tank as their own.

The reduced capacity of seawater to hold dissolved oxygen leads some to believe that a good baseline would be to cut the freshwater rule in half and aim for about one-half inch of fish per gallon of water. However, you should also consider the size of individual fish. According to this guideline, a 30-gallon (114-L) tank could hold about seven or eight 2-inch (5-cm) fish or one 15-inch (38-cm) fish. However, both will exceed the biological filtration and oxygen-carrying capacities of a 30-gallon tank (especially the 15-inch fish, which probably weighs as much as twenty 2-inch fish). Additionally, with the exception of some schooling species, many reef fish are too territorial to be packed this tightly together.

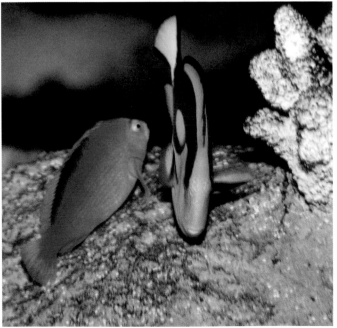

◐ A flame hawkfish and a hippo tang square off in a territorial dispute. As seen here, stiff body posture and flared fins are typical signs of aggression. Your tankmates' compatibility is one factor that will influence your tank size choice. If you keep aggressive species, you'll need to provide ample swimming space to avoid constant fighting.

A more realistic guideline is roughly one 2- to 3-inch (5- to 8-cm) fish per 5 to 10 gallons (19 to 38 L) of water, one 6-inch (15-cm) fish per 20 to 30 gallons (76 to 114 L), and so forth. Thus, a 30-gallon tank will hold three average-sized small fish; maybe four at the most. Except for some unusually aggressive species (such as many damselfishes and some dottybacks), your fish will have enough space to coexist without a great deal of conflict if you follow this equation.

SITING YOUR TANK

Where you want to put your aquarium will help determine such variables as your aquarium's size and shape. Select an aquarium to fit your space, not the reverse.

There are several important considerations when selecting the right place in your home for an aquarium. The most important consideration is weight; freshwater weighs approximately 8.3 pounds per gallon (3.8 kg per 3.8L), and seawater slightly more. There is also the weight of the tank itself, the stand or cabinet on which it sits, and the substrate and decorations inside. Therefore, you will want to place your aquarium where there is a stable floor to support it. Very large aquariums are inappropriate for upper floors of buildings. If you have any doubts whatsoever, consult a builder or structural engineer to guide you. In addition to a safe, stable floor on which to place the tank and its stand, examine other characteristics of the space. Avoid placing your aquarium in a sunny or brightly lit room; the excess light will make algae problems inevitable and will make viewing the inside of the tank difficult due to glare. You should also consider access to electrical outlets and allow adequate clearance for filters and lighting.

STANDS AND SUPPORT

An aquarium needs a sturdy stand. Adapting an existing piece of furniture, such as a coffee table, for use as an aquarium stand may work for small tanks but is not recommended. Most furniture, as sturdy as it may look, is not constructed to support the weight of a filled aquarium. A 30-gallon (114-L) aquarium, which would be considered small as marine aquariums go, could exceed 350 pounds (159 kg) when full of water, gravel, and decorations. A 125-gallon (473-L) aquarium could easily top half a ton! In addition, seawater will damage the finish of furniture that wasn't designed to take such abuse. So, it's definitely safer to buy a stand designed specifically for your tank.

SUBSTRATES

Your goals in selecting a substrate should be to have something that looks good, is not harmful to your aquarium animals, is chemically beneficial in terms of pH buffering, and is compatible with your fil-

⊖ Situate your aquarium on a sturdy stand such as this one.

ter (primarily a consideration if you use an undergravel system). An ideal substrate should also have a grain size that is large enough to keep it from compacting and "going anaerobic." A substrate with a grain size of less than 1 or 2 millimeters (mm) can develop spots where the oxygen is depleted and anaerobic bacteria grow. Although these bacteria are valuable and necessary to decompose and recycle dead organic material, they release hydrogen sulfide, a toxic gas that smells like rotten eggs. In a healthy, natural environment, this is not a problem—but in the aquarium, even a little bit of this gas can wipe out a tank of fish. Instead, you need to encourage the growth of aerobic nitrifying bacteria. These bacteria thrive in the presence of oxygen, and a substrate bed should have a massive colony of them, coating the grains of gravel. Each grain should be large enough (generally 3 to 5 mm) to permit water to flow freely and carry a rich supply of oxygen to the nitrifying bacteria.

Let's see if we can balance all of the chemical, environmental, and aesthetic qualities to select the right substrate for our needs. The commonly available marine substrate choices include: silica sand, dolomite, crushed coral, oyster shell, aragonite, and live sand. There are other substrates available, but for your first aquarium I would strongly recommend sticking with one of these choices, preferably aragonite or the more expensive live sand. Some experts are experimenting with other substrates, including even mud! The idea is usually to try reducing nitrates by deliberately encouraging controlled cultures of anaerobic bacteria, which convert nitrates to nitrogen gas that bubbles out of the water. However, these systems are tricky, prone to failure, and not recommended for your first time setting up a marine tank. Who knows? Twenty years from now we may all have mud-based substrates and filtration; but for now, stick to proven materials and methods. They're not perfect, but they will increase your chances of success.

Silica Sand

The same sort of sand you would use in a child's sandbox, silica sand is available at your local fish store. Although it is cheap and makes an attractive-looking substrate, it creates some difficult problems in a marine aquarium. First, it has little or no carbonate content, which means that it does nothing to buffer the pH of your water. Aquariums with a silica sand substrate will usually have problems with declining pH over the long haul. Second, silica sand is very abrasive. A handful of sand may feel soft, but if you looked at it under a microscope, you would see that the quartz grains actually have many sharp edges. Fish that do a lot of picking for food along the bottom or that dig or hide in the substrate will often develop bruises and abrasions, especially around the mouth. The sand will also scratch glass (if grains of sand are caught in an algae-scraping pad during your regular tank maintenance) and gouge acrylic tanks. Third, the sand is called "silica" because it contains a large amount of the element silicon (Si), which is used by some single-celled algae—diatoms—to construct their skeletons. With such a rich supply of the raw material needed for their growth, diatoms can "bloom" in a tank with a silica sand substrate, leading to unsightly and difficult-to-control brown or gold films on the glass and decorations. Although some tangs (surgeonfish) and snails will eat diatom films and give you some degree of biological control over these pests, most other marine animals won't touch them.

Calcareous Substrates

Calcareous substrates are composed primarily or entirely of calcium carbonate, which buffers pH to help maintain the necessary 8.0 to

8.4 range. However, just because a substrate contains this buffering compound does not mean that it actually buffers well in the aquarium. Confused? Don't be. It all has to do with crystals. Calcium carbonate ($CaCO_3$) is made up of tiny crystals, and different carbonate minerals have crystals of different shapes. The shapes of the crystals affect how well or how poorly their carbonate will dissolve in water—what buffering capacity is all about. Regardless of shape, some calcareous substrates are better than others, even though they may have the same chemical formula, $CaCO_3$.

Dolomite. Essentially crushed limestone, this is the substrate most often used in the early days of marine aquariums. It is still an acceptable substrate for fish-only aquariums, but it does have some drawbacks. First, it is fairly coarse-grained; this makes it a pretty good substrate for covering an undergravel filter, but it is too heavy and sharp for many sand-burrowing organisms. Many wrasses, for example, will scratch themselves, especially on the eyes, while attempting to burrow. Dolomite is also, well, kind of ugly—usually a medium gray color that doesn't look very natural in the aquarium. It is also a royal pain to clean before using; because it is a mined and processed mineral, it is very dusty and has to be rinsed. I'm telling you from experience that the first bucket of rinse water will look like milk! It takes many rinses before the water runs off clear and the dolomite is ready to place in the aquarium. Finally, although limestone is primarily calcium carbonate, dolomite has only a moderate pH-buffering capacity, and sometimes the pH has to drop below 8.0 to "activate" the dolomite.

Crushed coral. Crushed coral, like dolomite, is a fairly coarse gravel, although it is usually a bit less sharp-edged. Crushed coral is a calcite that has a crystal shape that makes it a relatively weak buffer. Both dolomite and crushed coral will probably require you to add supplemental buffering liquids or powders to maintain a stable, high pH. Crushed coral is whitish to light gray in color, usually paler than dolomite. Like

◐ Aragonite (top) and crushed coral (bottom) are two good options for aquarium substrate. Aragonite has a heftier price tag, but its chemical benefits such as a crystal structure that maintains a more stable pH make it worth your dollar.

dolomite, crushed coral is a mined mineral that requires a lot of rinsing before it can be used. The verdict? I like crushed coral a little better than dolomite, but not nearly as much as aragonite (see below).

Oyster shell. Oyster shell is a very inexpensive substrate that some aquarists have used with success, but it is another substrate I consider problematic. Unlike dolomite and crushed coral, oyster shell is usually not sold at your local fish store but is stocked by livestock feed suppliers as "shell grit." It is actually a supplement to chicken feed! Oyster shell is more attractive than dolomite or crushed coral because it has all the variegated colors of the shells that are crushed to make it: white, gray, black, blue, tan, and red. Unfortunately, the flat grains pack down over time and can trap uneaten food and other solid wastes, potentially creating a sanitation problem. It should not be used with undergravel filters because the flow rate through the gravel would be sluggish. Additionally, oyster shell is too smooth to provide a good surface for aerobic bacterial growth and doesn't buffer pH particularly well. Like the other substrates so far, it's also tedious to rinse before use.

Aragonite. Aragonite, often sold as "coral sand," should not be confused with crushed coral. Aragonite is a form of calcium carbonate with a crystal shape that enhances buffering capacity. In an aquarium that is not overstocked, aragonite will usually maintain a stable pH around 8.3. It maintains a high alkalinity, too, and significant levels of bioavailable calcium to support shell and skeletal growth in invertebrates. Additionally, it contains trace elements, such as strontium, that are usually lacking in the other calcareous substrates and are important to some invertebrates. The downside is that aragonite is more expensive than the other calcareous substrates and takes just as long to wash. However, it is still a step up in quality.

Live sand. Live sand is wet aragonite that contains thriving colonies of aerobic bacteria. Some of this is "wild" sand, but more often it is aragonite mined in tropical coastal locations and cultured in controlled systems to develop colonies of nitrifying bacteria before it is bagged and shipped. This is, hands down, the premium substrate on the market today, but it is pricey. Because it is shipped in bags with water, the extra weight adds to the shipping cost and the final price; it also means that a bag of, say, 25 pounds (11 kg) probably only contains about 20 pounds (9 kg) of sand and about 5 pounds (2 kg) of water. On top of that, the sand has a limited shelf life, generally about a year, so a bag of live sand will have an expiration date. The good thing, though, is that you don't have to wash it. In fact, you never want to wash it because you'd be rinsing away the bacteria that you paid extra to get! Some aquarists may pass on live sand and go with one of the other substrates, and I am not about to claim you can't be successful that way. However, I am more than

◉ Live sand contains active nitrifying bacteria colonies that can substantially reduce the "run-in" time of the initial nitrogen cycle in a new aquarium.

willing to spend the extra money on live sand because it is a more attractive product, has better chemical properties, and jump-starts the process of cycling a new aquarium.

Live sand and dry aragonite are sold in a variety of grades, and this adds to the possibilities for the marine aquarist. There are types that have lots of shell fragments and even small whole seashells, others that approximate the pink sands of South Pacific islands, and even some that contain black sand like the famed volcanic beaches of Hawaii. You can use a single type, or you can mix them to create a variety of colors and textures.

TEMPERATURE

Depending on its location in your home, your aquarium will almost certainly need a heater. Heaters are available in a wide range of prices, but I advise you not to purchase an extremely cheap one. Inexpensive heaters have a nasty tendency to occasionally get stuck in the *on* position, cooking everything in the tank. More expensive heaters have electronic thermostats that are more reliable. You'll want to aim for a temperature in the range of 74 to 78 degrees Fahrenheit (23 to 26 degrees Celsius) for most tropical marine fish, preferably at the lower end of this range. Anything exceeding 80°F (26°C) would be considered the danger zone for all but the hardiest of tropical marine fish.

If you find that you consistently have a problem maintaining a temperature below 80°F (26°C), you may need to consider a chiller unit. This is a small refrigeration system that cools the water; some need an external pump to move water through the unit, and others just have a titanium cylinder that is placed inside the tank. Chillers are often needed for reef aquariums because the high-intensity lighting they use heats the water, but it would be rare for a fish-only

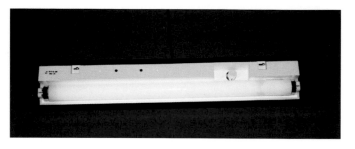

➲ This simple strip-style light should suffice for your basic marine aquarium. Install a timer to ensure your tropical fish receive about twelve hours of light per day.

tank to have this problem unless it happened to be placed in a room with poor circulation and no air conditioning (not recommended!).

LIGHTING

You'll find a million opinions on what constitutes the "best" lighting system for the marine aquarium, with calculations of watts-per-gallon and such. If you scan aquarium books and magazines and visit your local fish store, you will see many lighting options, including incandescent, fluorescent, high-output fluorescent, actinic, metal halide, and more. Some are very expensive, to boot. Having light of the correct intensity and spectrum is important for keeping photosynthetic animals, such as corals, as well as some (but not all) marine plants; however, in this book we will not go into the details of lighting for those organisms, which are really more for reef tanks. As previously mentioned, I believe we should keep it simple for your first marine aquarium, which means avoiding all photosynthetic invertebrates and most plants.

For fish-only tanks or, at the most, tanks containing a combination of fish and non-photosynthetic invertebrates such as crustaceans, a simple fluorescent full hood (a two-piece unit available at your local fish store) or a glass aquarium top and a strip-style fluorescent light will do just fine. Most of these are in the range of 20 to 40 watts per fluorescent tube, depending on length. A standard 48-inch (122-cm) tube, for example, is rated for 40 watts. For wider and/or deeper tanks, two-tube light fixtures are available.

Because I'm assuming that your first marine tank will probably be a tropical one, your fish will be approximately equatorial in origin. The day and night are roughly of equal length at the Equator, so your lights should be on for approximately twelve hours per day. I suggest that you use an inexpensive timer to turn them on and off.

FILTRATION: YOUR AQUARIUM'S LIFE-SUPPORT SYSTEM

Filters are essential to keeping the water clean and well-supplied with oxygen. Without an efficient filter or combination of filters, every organism in a marine aquarium could die in as little as a few hours or days. However, filtration is another aspect of marine aquarium-keeping that is always controversial. There are dozens of different filter types available and no end of theories on the best ways to use them, either alone or in combination. Many books and magazine articles have attempted to define the "perfect" filtration system. Although I'm sure that many experts will disagree with me, I'm here to tell you that there is no such thing. Particular filtration approaches may often work better for one type of aquarium versus another (for example, in a fish-only aquarium versus an invertebrate-packed reef aquarium), but I have yet to see one filter device or filtration approach that will work for all marine aquariums under all conditions. I hope to cut through the confusion rather than add to it. Let's look first at what we are trying to accomplish with filtration, and then examine some of the most popular filter systems and how they will help us reach those goals.

It is possible to spend as little as just a few dollars on a simple filter, and hundreds or thousands of dollars on larger, complex systems—but all complete filter systems combine mechanical, chemical, and biological filtration. Mechanical filtration is simply the removal of large particles such as uneaten food, solid fish wastes (okay, fish poop), and sediment. Chemical filtration uses media such as activated carbon to absorb potentially harmful chemicals from the water. Finally, biological filtration uses living organisms—specifically, the nitrifying bacteria that drive the nitrogen cycle—to transform nitrogenous fish wastes (okay, fish pee) into less harmful substances.

Let's look at some popular and successful filter types and how well each one performs these three functions.

Sponge Filters

At the low-tech end of the scale in filtration is the very inexpensive sponge filter. A sponge filter is little more than a large block of open-cell polyurethane foam, into which a slotted plastic cylinder is inserted. A length of airline tubing runs down into the cylinder; the other end is attached to a vibrator air pump outside the aquarium. As it bubbles out of the cylinder, the air creates a current that draws water through the sponge. On the microscopic level, the sponge has a tremendous amount of surface area for bacteria to colonize, but it takes a while for them to build up to useful levels—probably several weeks. However, once a sponge filter is well-colonized, it is a good mechanical filter, trapping particulate matter in the sponge foam, and an excellent biological filter with a large capacity to convert toxic ammonium. However, most sponge filter designs do not include activated carbon or other chemical filter media; so, if it is the only filter in a tank, you will need to do water changes to compensate.

Maintaining a sponge filter is easy, if somewhat messy. Periodically, just remove it from the tank and squeeze it out repeatedly in a bucket of clean seawater, then put it back in the tank and reattach the airline. This will flush out a good deal of the collected gunk (okay, mostly fish poop) but without liberating too many of the nitrifying bacteria. Whatever you do, never rinse out a sponge filter in freshwater or you'll kill the bacteria you worked so hard to culture.

Sponge Filter

In truth, the sponge filter is best for a quarantine aquarium, where we can't have activated carbon or other chemical filter media that might remove medications. In display aquariums, they tend to be large and unsightly. There is no reason that sponge filters couldn't be used as add-on filtration for a display tank, but I have rarely seen it done.

Undergravel Filters

For many years, undergravel filters were the workhorses of both marine and freshwater aquariums. These filters consist of a perforated plastic plate that covers the entire bottom of an aquarium and is buried under a deep (usually 2 to 3 inches [5 to 8 cm]) gravel bed, with cylindrical lift tubes in the rear corners. The operating principle is similar to that of the sponge filter: airline tubing is attached to an airstone (a porous wood, silica, or plastic "stone" that creates fine bubbles when air is pumped through it) that is placed into each lift tube, near the tubes' bases. As air is bubbling upward in the lift tubes, it creates a suction that draws water down through the gravel bed and up and out of the lift tubes. Recently, aquarists have discovered the efficiency of undergravel filters was increased by mounting a powerhead (a small submersible water pump) at the top of each lift tube, which created more powerful water flow through the gravel bed.

Undergravel filters have the advantage of having a truly massive area for bacterial colonization. The entire substrate of the aquarium becomes one huge filter, and every grain of gravel is home to nitrifying bacteria. The disadvantage is that the entire substrate is also a giant particulate filter. Solid wastes are trapped between the gravel grains, and if they are not removed periodically they can completely fill in the spaces between the gravel grains, choking off the flow of water and leading to the formation of anaerobic "dead zones." Thus, it's important to regularly remove the accumulated gunk with a gravel-vacuuming siphon hose. Using a supplemental power filter as a particulate filter can help, but it won't eliminate this problem completely. An ingenious attempt to do an end-run around the problem was the reverse-flow undergravel filter, which used powerheads to pump water down the lift tubes and up through the gravel bed to reduce particulate clogging. Why this never caught on is a mystery to me. It seemed like a good idea.

So, should you consider an undergravel filter? Most people today would say no, and they do have a case. It just isn't possible to completely eliminate clogging. As months and even years go by, the waste matter will build up. It may not build up to dangerous levels, but it will insidiously create a nutrient overload that can fuel algae blooms. After a few years, most marine tanks that employ an undergravel as the primary filter will develop chronic algae problems. Eventually, the tank just looks so ugly that the discouraged hobbyist just takes it down and sells everything in the local classifieds. Undergravels work, but the maintenance is a chore that will probably get away from you despite your best intentions.

Undergravel Filter

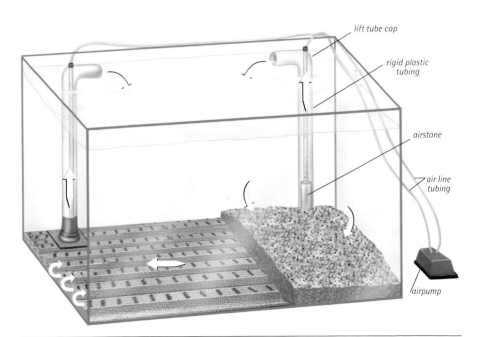

lift tube cap

rigid plastic tubing

airstone

air line tubing

airpump

Power Filters

Most filters have "power" somewhere, but the term *power filter* is most commonly used to describe a plastic box filter than hangs on the back of an aquarium and uses a magnetically driven impeller to pump water up, out of the aquarium, and into the filter box, where it is passed through filter pads, probably through a layer of activated carbon, and maybe through an optional insert containing some type of biological filter medium such as ceramic "noodles."

I have mixed feelings about these filters, although I have used and continue to use them for various applications. They are good at particulate filtration, fair at chemical filtration, and good to poor at biological filtration, depending on specific design elements of various brands. For me, a major advantage is that it is very easy to change the filter media, usually without disconnecting the filter. These filters are also very aerobic, with good flow, ensuring that all the media in the box get plenty of oxygen. A disadvantage is that most designs hold relatively small amounts of filter media, so pads, carbon, etc., must be replaced frequently. On the other hand, because the easy access makes swapping filter media easy, I like to use chemical media such as phosphate-absorbing or nitrate-absorbing "pillows" that would be hard to replace in any other type of filter.

Power Filter

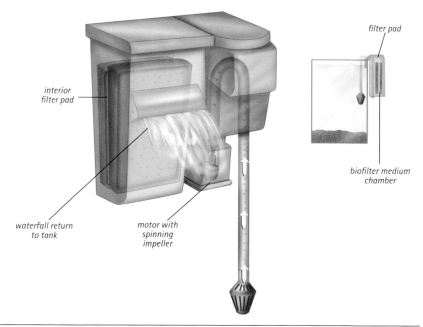

filter pad

interior filter pad

biofilter medium chamber

waterfall return to tank

motor with spinning impeller

Another disadvantage of power filters, however, is that most models have a lid that fits relatively loosely on top of the filter, which lets spray dry and build crusty masses of salt ("salt creep") around the edges of the filter box.

Canister Filters

Canister filters are large, freestanding power filters with a motor that sits atop a large container that is usually compartmentalized for various filter media. The canister is sealed with an O-ring, and hoses feed water into the canister from the bottom and return it from the top to the aquarium via an aerating spray bar. Depending on the filter design, the water usually passes first through a layer of a mechanical filtration medium, such as coarse foam; then through a biological medium with a large surface area, such as specially manufactured ceramic "noodles;" and finally through a layer of chemical medium, such as activated carbon.

Canister Filter

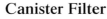

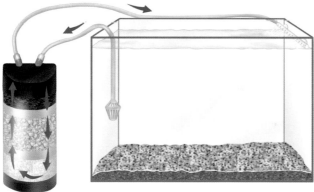

Canister filters have several advantages. They hold large amounts of filter media, they have powerful motors that create good flow and aeration; they are usually very quiet, and they are generally placed out of sight inside the aquarium's cabinet stand.

However, over time they will tend to clog up, and the flow rate from the spray bar will noticeably decrease. When this happens, the filter has to be disconnected from the tank. This will be much easier if you purchase the optional valves that let you disconnect the filter without removing all the hosing from the tank. The filter can be back-flushed to remove the clogging debris but, because this has to be done with seawater to avoid killing the bacteria, you will probably end up just opening the filter and removing the trays of filter media to rinse the biological media in a bucket of seawater and completely replace the activated carbon. In other words, canister filters are large, efficient, and powerful, but servicing them can be a hassle.

The other thing I don't like about canister filters is that many of them are not self-priming. They use a gravity feed; in other words, you have to suck on the outlet hose to get a siphon of water started to fill the canister, and quickly reconnect the outlet hose to the spray bar while the canister is filling. Only then can you plug in the filter.

Still, canister filters are probably the single most frequent choice for fish-only marine aquariums, and they have proven their reliability.

Trickle Filters

Trickle filters, sometimes called "wet-dry" filters, employ a large filter box, usually made of acrylic, which is placed under the aquarium. Water enters a reservoir or sump on one side of the filter, where a submersible motor pumps a spray of water over plastic "bio-balls." The bio-balls are constructed to have many surfaces and interior chambers, and serve as the medium on which the nitrifying bacteria grow. Because the bio-balls are not underwater, but have a well-aerated mixture of air and water sprayed over them at all times, they are an extremely good aerobic medium for bacterial growth and cycling of nitrogenous wastes. The sump of the filter is also a good place to put heaters, protein skimmers, and other equipment that may be a tad more unsightly if just hung on the tank.

The advantage of trickle filters is that they do an extremely good job of biological filtration. For this reason alone, they are the choice of many serious marine hobbyists, including most folks who keep reef tanks. However, they are not sealed, and some designs may be prone to overflowing, which creates quite a mess. If you opt for a trickle filter, make sure you understand the directions for using it.

Live Rock and Live Sand

Live rock and live sand are substrate and decorative materials that we'll consider in more detail in the Aquascaping Decorations section shortly following, but they are decorations that carry a heavy load of nitrifying bacteria; so, if you opt for using them, they are actually part of your filter system. Most experienced aquarists recommend about 1 pound (454 g) of live sand or 1 to 1.5 pounds (454 to 680 g) of live rock per gallon (3.8 L) of water. Be sure to use only cured live rock for your first attempt. This is rock that has been collected and placed in circulating, filtered, artificial seawater (such as found at your local fish store or a holding facility) to allow anything that has died on it to release its decomposition products before it is placed in your tank. If you use uncured rock, you could end up with a smelly mess.

Live rock and live sand basically allow you to place a functioning biological filter in your tank much more quickly than it would take

◉ Shown here is a sample of Fijian live rock.

to culture the bacteria the old-fashioned way; that is, adding a handful of gravel from an established tank and then stocking damselfish or mollies. However, you still will often get an ammonium reading for at least a few days before the new live rock/sand stabilizes. So, it isn't quite an "instant" system, although it is often portrayed as one.

My own preference (and I am sure I will get some disagreement on this) is to do your first tank the old-fashioned way (but with the hardier mollies, not the less robust damsels). It's cheaper and it's tried and true.

Protein Skimmers

A protein skimmer is a device that hardly looks like a filter. It usually consists of a tall, cylindrical column that draws water from the tank and swirls it around with extremely fine bubbles; sometimes the bubbles come from a simple airstone, and sometimes they are injected by more complicated mechanisms.

A protein skimmer is designed to remove waste proteins and other large molecules from the water. If not removed, they build up over time, even if you do regular water changes. The skimmer makes use of an oddity of long-chain molecules such as proteins: they have hydrophilic (attracted to water) and hydrophobic (repelled by water) ends. When a bubble of air passes by, a protein molecule will stick its hydrophobic "tail" into the bubble to get it into the air and away from the water. A bubble will pick up many protein molecules and drag them along to the surface of the filter column. At the top of a protein skimmer, the bubbles will create a dry, yellowish, or brownish foam (of proteins and other large molecules) that collects in a removable cup.

Protein Skimmer

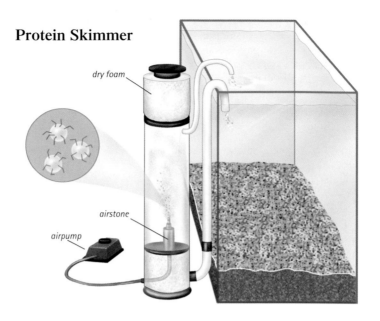

dry foam

airstone

airpump

Different skimmers have various innovations that swirl the air bubbles or recirculate the water to maximize the contact time between air and water—and the more innovative, the more expensive, generally speaking. However, there are skimmers sized for every marine aquarium, and you should have one; once considered more or less an option for the marine aquarium, there is now nearly universal agreement that no marine aquarium should be without a protein skimmer. In fact, some hobbyists have created successful marine tanks with nothing more than live rock and a skimmer, and no other filtration! I don't recommend that you try to do this (it's tricky!), but it just goes to show that the mechanical/chemical filtration of a skimmer and the biological filtration of live rock can create a viable system all by themselves.

Ultraviolet Sterilizers

An ultraviolet (UV) sterilizer is an opaque cylinder containing a tube that emits ultraviolet radiation to kill free-floating viruses, bacteria, and parasites. It's more of a filter accessory than a true filter—it is placed in the middle of the return flow to an aquarium from a trickle or canister filter.

A UV sterilizer is an optional piece of equipment. If you select fish carefully, quarantine them before adding them to an established aquarium, and maintain high water quality in your aquarium, it should not be necessary to have this expensive piece of equipment to kill disease bugs in the water. Additionally, you need to know that the radiation output of the tube drops off long before the tube actually burns out. Most manufacturers recommend replacing the tube about every six months, and they aren't cheap.

I don't mean to sound as if I'm against using UV sterilizers. In fact, if you are going to keep extremely rare, expensive, and delicate fish, a sterilizer may provide you with an extra safety margin you'll be thankful for. For example, I know a number of hobbyists who keep rare butterflyfish and angelfish, and, since these species are rather prone to unusual bacterial infections and protozoan parasites, their keepers swear by UV sterilizers.

AQUASCAPING DECORATIONS

The term *aquascaping* was coined to describe the aquatic counterpart of landscaping; that is, the arrangement of decorations to provide a natural-looking and attractive display that also provides the fish and other denizens of your tank with the shelter and security they need.

Coral Skeletons

When I first started out in the marine hobby some years ago (I won't say how many!), pretty much the only decorative options available were dead, bleached, white coral skeletons. Some of us thought that was the way corals were supposed to look! Today, these are still available, but conscientious hobbyists should avoid them because they represent an ecologically irresponsible harvesting of a resource that regenerates very slowly (see Coral Regeneration box). In places such as the Philippines, reefs are hacked, chopped, and blasted to provide

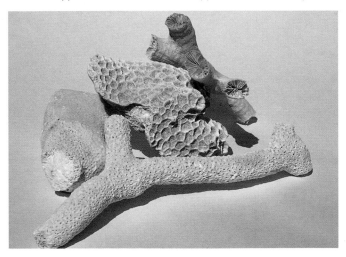

◑ This sample of bleached coral doesn't spice up an aquarium as do the vibrantly colored coral replicas available nowadays. Because of the methods used to harvest live corals, the resource's regeneration process is slow— another reason to purchase only artificial corals.

coral heads that are then bleached white and sold on the curio market—and some of these, regrettably, also make their way into the aquarium trade. Even without considering the ecological effects, there is a very practical reason for avoiding bleached, dead corals. They are algae magnets! They are prone to developing thick, noxious growth of hair algae or the blue-green bacteria often called "slime algae." Despite their carbonate content, dead corals also do little to buffer pH; in fact, natural or added buffers in seawater may precipitate out of the solution and bind to the coral skeletons. The bottom line? Don't buy them, and encourage your local fish store not to stock them.

Coral Replicas

In the "old days," little did we know that live corals come in as many colors as fish. Many live corals are shades of green, gold, or brown, thanks to symbiotic algae called zooxanthellae in their tissues; but there are also species that are blue, pink, purple, orange, or just about any other color. Thankfully, we now have access to artificial corals that look like the real thing, and they even come in dozens of shapes, sizes, and colors that look much better than those dead corals we used to use. These may be molded out of vinyl, polyurethane, various plastics, or ceramics. They are also somewhat

○ Fluorescent artificial corals add a splash of color to your aquascaping design. Although they appear gaudy, many of these actually are a good approximation of the real colors of living corals.

less expensive than coral skeletons, and you can buy them without guilt. The best part, though, is that we can finally make a very realistic-looking reef environment for our fish.

Plants

There are a few live plants—specifically, larger algae species called "macroalgae"—that you may wish to consider for your marine aquarium. Chief among these are the green algae of the genus *Caulerpa*. These are usually feathery in appearance, growing from a creeping rhizome that looks like a root (technically, they're not roots because

◐ Living corals come in a variety of colors—green, gold, brown, pink, blue— that modern artificial corals duplicate well.

CORAL REGENERATION

Living coral grows very slowly. Although the actual growth rates depend on variables such as sunlight, temperature, and available nutrients, the yearly growth of many tropical corals is in the range of about one-quarter to 1 inch (5 to 25 mm). Therefore, the massive coral heads seen on many tropical reefs may be centuries old, and the reefs themselves are 5,000 to 10,000 years old. Even the fastest-growing corals on record (some of the *Acropora* species) do not exceed 8 inches (20 cm) per year. For comparison, many coral reef fish reach maturity in a little as 1 or 2 years. Therefore, the harvesting of corals as curios or for the aquarium trade is ethically questionable at best because it may take many years for new corals to grow to take the place of those that were harvested.

◗ Macroalgae are useful in tanks with herbivorous fish species such as tangs (family Acanthuridae).

they only serve to anchor the plant and don't supply water and nutrients as do the true roots of more advanced plants). *Caulerpa* are attractive and easy to grow. In fact, many species grow like wildfire, and you will need to prune them often to keep them from getting out of control, or you'll need plant-eating fish such as tangs. *Caulerpa* also have a ravenous appetite for iron, a necessary nutrient for their growth, and they will quickly absorb all the iron that is normally available as a trace element in your artificial seawater. When that happens, they may suddenly "crash," dying off in as little as several days and perhaps making the whole tank crash, too. Iron additives are available at your local fish store to replace what the algae remove, but in most cases I think that it's best to avoid live macroalgae for your first marine tank. However, if you are a serious fan of tangs or other herbivorous fish, it may be worth the effort to grow macroalgae so that your fish have a constant food supply.

If you enjoy the appearance of plants but not the hassle and risk involved with culturing live ones, artificials are now available in plastic or fabric. Like the corals, there are many species, colors, and sizes available, and they look surprisingly real.

Live Rock

I've saved the best—and most controversial—for last. Live rock is undoubtedly the favorite aquascaping material available because it provides shelter, a base for constructing more elaborate aquascapes (particularly in reef aquariums), and a source of nitrifying bacteria. In fact, the "live rock method" is a form of filtration unto itself, as we have seen. But just what is live rock? Live rocks are loose stones or boulders harvested from sand flats or rubble piles at the bases of reefs. These rocks typically have no live corals attached, but they have a lot of encrusting algae, sponges, hydroids, and hitchhikers (such as small crabs), and a large amount of aerobic bacteria. The quality and price of live rock will vary depending on where it's harvested. For example, Caribbean live rock is generally considered lower quality but is relatively cheap. At the other end of the scale is live rock from locations such as Fiji and Tonga, which is considered high quality but also comes with a premium price.

Is harvesting live rock damaging to natural habitats? This is not an easy question to answer, but it's a question I think we have to ask. I don't claim to be an expert, but I have tried to consider it objectively and, in my estimation, live rock is a renewable resource if it is not overharvested. The places where storms and currents accumulate the rubble piles that become "live" over time will continue to accumulate new rock as it is knocked free of the reef. So, new rock should continue to replace rock that is harvested as long as it isn't harvested by the boatload. Additionally, conscientious collectors of both live rock and fish make an effort to rotate collecting areas so that they will not place too much collecting pressure on any one area.

A commodity that is developing slowly, but will hopefully become more important in the future, is aquacultured live rock. In particular, some Florida entrepreneurs are using this method. Unprocessed limestone is obtained from inland sources, broken into suitably sized pieces, and transported to offshore beds leased from the state. The rock is tagged for licensing and ownership purposes and is placed on the seafloor. Soon, algae, encrusting invertebrates, and aerobic bacteria will colonize the rock. How long the rock is left on the bottom is variable, but it is often six months to a year.

⊖ This Fijian live rock is somewhat pricier than Caribbean versions; you may feel the higher quality is worth the price. Combined with a live sand substrate, the bacteria on live rock help break down the nitrogen-based waste products of fish and other organisms.

➔ Arrange your tank with larger decorations in back and smaller accessories in front.

Placement

Arranging the various decorative materials to create a pleasing aquascape is an art that will probably take you some time to develop, and I'm not the judge of all that is tasteful and lovely in an aquarium. In the end, you should arrange the decorations so that they look good to you, and then observe your fish and other animals to evaluate whether they at ease (uncomfortable animals are skittish). However, I can offer you a few tips that have usually worked for me: First, as a general rule, build your aquascaping so that taller or larger decorations are placed toward the back wall of the tank, with shorter or smaller items placed toward the front. However, don't build the aquascaping all the way to the front glass. Most fish need shelter, but they also require some open swimming room.

Second, use a variety of colors and textures of decorations; for example, a plate coral placed horizontally to provide shelter for nocturnal fish, a tall staghorn coral for the hawkfish that likes to take a high perch, and darker base rocks to create caves and crevices. Finally, make your aquascape as complex as possible, with many nooks and crannies. This will give your fish places to hide and will also reduce territorial aggression.

ASSEMBLY

When the aquarium is placed on its stand and is situated in the most attractive and practical location, use a bubble level on all four sides to make sure the tank is level. This is especially important with glass tanks; when they are not level, excessive pressure could be exerted on one side or a corner and, in a worst-case scenario, the tank could leak, crack, or even shatter. I don't want to scare you here; the odds of this happening are remote, but why take the chance when it's easy to level the tank while it's still empty?

When the tank is situated, stable, and level, add the substrate you've selected. If you are using an undergravel filter, you will need a substrate layer at least 2 inches (5 cm) deep; if you are relying on external filtration—power, canister, or trickle—you can use a shallower substrate, perhaps only 1 inch (2.5 cm). A shallow substrate layer will have less a tendency to develop dead spots, but it will also limit you somewhat in your choice of fish and other creatures. Animals that like to dig—such as jawfish, some gobies, and many crustaceans—will need a deeper substrate of 2 inches (5 cm) or more. Fortunately, their digging behavior moves the substrate constantly and helps keep dead spots from forming. I guess that's compensation for their disruption of your carefully sculpted aquascape!

Next, fill the tank slowly with artificial seawater that you've mixed to the proper specific gravity (1.022 to 1.023) in a separate container (see Tank Monitoring in Chapter 3 for more details about specific gravity). I don't recommend that you add freshwater to your tank and then add the salt—which is especially vital if you are using live sand and/or live rock. You'll kill the bacteria if they are exposed to freshwater or to wild fluctuations in salinity. The water needs to be of the correct specific gravity, pH, and temperature before you expose the bacterial colonies to it. Even if you're not using live rock/live sand, it is easier to mix seawater in a bare container, such as a bare aquarium, to make sure that it dissolves completely and you get an accurate reading of specific gravity. If you mix your water in the display tank, you may have a much higher reading the next day due to carbonates and other components that dissolve slowly.

When the tank is filled about halfway, add your aquascaping materials—live rock (if applicable) or base rock and coral replicas. Take some time to arrange them to your liking. You can certainly rearrange them once the tank is full, but you get wetter doing it, so why not take your time while the tank's only half full?

Fill the tank the rest of the way, then attach the heater, filter, and skimmer, but don't plug anything in yet. Prime the filter if necessary. Place the tank cover and light.

Now you can start to plug things in. Start with the filter and skimmer. Make sure they're running and you get a good, strong flow from the return. Next, plug in the heater. Adjust until the pilot light just comes on. Check it periodically over the next couple of days, and turn it up or down slightly until the temperature is stable. Finally, turn on the light and enjoy your handiwork. Soon you'll be ready to add your first fish.

But not too soon! We have already discussed the nitrogen cycle (and see Tank Monitoring in Chapter 3 for more details), and it may take you a few days to several weeks of monitoring the levels of ammonium, nitrite, and nitrate before your aquarium is ready for its first permanent residents. You should have nothing more exotic than a molly in the tank until the ammonium and nitrite are reading zero!

Step 1: Position the tank and stand. Make sure the tank is level.

Step 2: Cut and attach background to tank with clear tape.

Step 3: Add your substrate.

Step 4: Mix seawater in a separate container.

During this time you should also be checking the pH and making sure it is stable at 8.2 to 8.4. Keep checking the temperature, too. You want to make sure that every physical and chemical factor you can easily measure is stable and within the accepted normal range before you add that first "real" fish.

Step 5: Fill tank halfway.

Step 6: Add artificial corals and/or live rock and other decor. Top off tank's water level.

Step 7: Attach filter, heater, and protein skimmer

Step 8: Add top and light.

Stocking and Maintaining
Your Aquarium and Fish

Your tank is finally cycled, ammonia and nitrite levels are reading zero, pH is in the zone, and specific gravity and temperature are on the money. Congratulations! You are now ready to add your first "real" fish (not counting those you may have used to cycle the tank). I don't want to scare you, but the next few choices you make can spell the difference between success and failure for this whole venture!

Selecting the right fish for an aquarium is an art form, and it takes experience. I've had decades of experience in selecting fish, both marine and freshwater, but I still don't always get it right. Proper fish selection depends on several vital factors, including the overall health of a fish at the time of purchase, its habitat requirements, its dietary needs, its compatibility with the other fish, and perhaps invertebrates that it will have to interact with in the aquarium. Let's look at how you can make intelligent evaluations of these factors.

BUYING FISH

It is important to understand that all fish experience some degree of stress in being shipped to your local fish store. The vast majority of marine fish are wild-caught; even when this is done in an environmentally sensitive way, without chemicals, and with gentle handling, there is stress involved from being netted, brought to the surface, and transported to shore. There is additional stress from shipping: being bagged up, placed in a box, bounced around, placed on a plane, and shipped perhaps halfway around the globe. Therefore, newly arrived fish need some time to adjust to their new surroundings when they arrive at your local fish store. It is unwise to purchase a fish that is fresh off the plane, and most stores won't sell them right out of the box. It is better to let them settle in for a few days before taking them home. If you see a fish you really want and you are afraid someone else will buy it first, ask the proprietor to put it on hold for you. You may need to place a small deposit on it but virtually every local fish store I have ever seen has an on hold policy. Don't forget to ask about the store's policy on what happens if, in a worst-case situation, the fish dies while it is on hold. If you've placed a deposit on it, you should get your money back, but confirm this up front. You should also determine the store's policy on losses after you take a fish home. Many stores have a refund policy for losses occurring during a specified period (often twenty-four hours, but sometimes up to a week);

however, there is often a stipulation that you need to bring in a water sample to prove that your water quality was within normal limits.

Try to buy "teenage" fish when possible. With many species, a curious fact is that very small juveniles and large, full-grown adults are often less adaptable to captive life than specimens that are somewhere in-between—the "teenagers," if you will. So, if a particular species reaches a maximum length of 6 inches (15.2 cm), for example, the ideal size to buy would be 3 or 4 inches (7.6 to 10.2 cm). Avoid the 1-inch (2.5 cm) babies and 6-inch oldsters.

You also need to select a mix of fish that will get along well in the same tank. Let's start with a basic truth: big fish eat little fish. Remember that and you've already mastered about 90 percent of what it takes to assemble a compatible mix of fish in your aquarium. Almost any fish, even of a species that is not normally a fish eater, will eat a smaller fish if it can. Pay attention to the sizes of fish mouths! There is also territoriality to consider. Ironically, most marine fish

◓ Fish collected from the ocean are likely to be stressed; not only are they suddenly in a new environment, they also endure stressful transport to your local fish store. Gentle handling is critical to helping them adapt to aquarium life.

don't like others of their own species (we call these conspecifics). Many freshwater fish are territorial, too—ask anyone who keeps cichlids—but marine fish take it to the extreme. Why? It's probably because resources are limited on the coral reef. No doubt you've seen photos or video of multitudes of colorful fish flocking over the reef; those images are probably part of the reason you're reading this book. You want to recreate that paradise in your own home, right? The problem is that it isn't a paradise. Those fish are all competing for their own little bit of space on a reef with untold millions of other fish that also need that space. Reef fish are engineered by nature to be aggressive because they have to fight to survive—competing for space, food, mates, etc.—all the while trying not to end up on some larger creature's menu. If you're a reef fish such as an angelfish, to pick just one example, a conspecific on your turf represents the worst sort of threat because it wants exactly what you want—the same food, the same shelter, and your mate(s). You can't blame a fish for acting aggressively to that threat.

In fact, in many reef fish (and angelfish include some of the best examples), juveniles and adults have strikingly different color patterns. Many ichthyologists believe that the colors of juveniles are meant to defuse aggression from adults; in other words, "I don't look like you, so I'm not your enemy."

The bottom line is that with many reef fish species, you will only be able to keep one individual per species per tank. In general, it's safer to assume that this is necessary than it is to assume the opposite. As we get into the discussion of the various species that follow, I'll get more specific about which are more aggressive and which are more peaceful.

ACCLIMATION

When you bring a fish home from your local fish store, regardless of whether you are adding it to your display tank or to a quarantine tank (see Chapter 5 for details), it must be done slowly. Transport is stressful, and so is adjusting to a new environment and new water that is probably slightly different in salinity, temperature, and pH. Do not just float the transport bag in the new aquarium for fifteen minutes and then just dump the fish out. In fact, I don't float the bag at all. I carefully cut the bag and place the new fish and all of its transport water into a small plastic bucket (be sure you use one that is only used for aquarium purposes).

Next, I take about a 6-foot (183-cm) piece of airline tubing and snake it into the aquarium. A gentle inhale starts a siphon of water flowing from the aquarium into the bucket. I use the aquarium lid to gently hold and slightly pinch the airline tubing so that the flow of water into the bucket is only a few drops per second. The water from the tank very gradually mixes with the transport water, and the new fish very gradually acclimates to the new water conditions. If you do it right, it should take about an hour.

Because I don't want any of the transport water, I then gently net the fish out of the bucket and place it in its new tank. Then, it's lights out. Fish acclimate better with the lights off. Additionally, I do not attempt to feed the new fish for at least twenty-four hours, sometimes even forty-eight hours if it acts skittish with the lights on.

FEEDING FISH

Feeding marine fish properly can be easy or challenging, depending on the species. Some fish are eager to eat immediately after being released from their shipping bags, whereas others will only slowly begin to take food in captivity, and some will not feed at all and slowly starve to death. We want to do everything we can to avoid

◉ These yellow tangs—which are herbivorous fish—nibble on a fresh broccoli crown.

A yellow-headed eel snags a goldfish.

that last situation, and it starts with doing your research before buying a fish. Do you know what it eats in the wild? Can you provide that food, or something close to it? Some foods, such as the live coral polyps that are the diet of some butterflyfish, just can't be provided in enough quantity to keep a delicate specimen fed. Therefore, the first step to feeding fish is to keep only those species that will eat in captivity.

It is also important to know not only what a fish eats, but how it eats—how often, how much, and what size. Many reef fish—such as damselfish, butterflyfish, angelfish, tangs, and most other species with small mouths—are basically grazers that pick at small food items almost all day long. Other species, such as lionfish and groupers, take large prey intermittently and may not hunt successfully every day. Try

FOOD, STRESS, AND ACCLIMATION

Even with careful handling, a fish will be stressed by transport to your home and introduction to its new environment. Stressed fish often will not eat; so, you should never attempt to feed a new fish on its first day in your tank. Acclimate it carefully as previously described, turn out the lights, and leave the fish in peace for at least the first twenty-four hours. After that, you can attempt to feed it. Be prepared to try more than one type of food. Don't be upset if a fish refuses all foods for the first few days. If the fish is healthy, water conditions are good, and you are offering appropriate foods, the fish should eventually begin to pick at foods, and you can gradually offer larger quantities and a wider variety.

to adapt your feeding schedule to the habits of your fish, perhaps offering the grazers small (and I mean *small*—a pinch between your thumb and forefinger is the right amount) quantities of food three or four times a day and offering the large predators chunky foods no more than every other day.

Variety is the spice of life, it's said, and that was never truer than here. Offer your fish as many different items as they will accept. Be careful not to overfeed, but at the same time make sure that all your fish get enough to eat. A greedy eater can sometimes consume all the foods before other fish can get to it. It is not uncommon to have obese fish and starving fish in the same tank because of differences in feeding behavior, so try to make sure your specimens all have similar feeding behavior, or make a special effort to get food to the less assertive individuals (which may mean driving away the aggressive feeders). Be sure that grazers have small amounts of food offered at least three times a day or available constantly in the form of a nori seaweed leaf or other vegetable matter. On the other hand, make sure that the predators do not get too much to eat. If you take care to make sure that you offer appropriate foods—of appropriate size, in appropriate amounts, at appropriate intervals, and appropriate to your fish inhabitants' behavior—you will be able to sustain many marine fish species happily for many years in the aquarium.

Let's take a look at some of the foods available to you from your local fish store or supermarket. These are by no means the only foods you can try, but I hope to give you a good variety of choices so that you will have something to offer even the most finicky feeder.

◔ "Feeder" goldfish are readily available at any pet store, but they may not be the best food option for predatory fish. Feeder fish often are kept in crowded store tanks, risking the spread of disease and parasites. Ultimately, this increases the chance that your fish may become ill, too.

Feeder Fish

Goldfish, guppies, and "rosy reds" (a gold form of the fathead minnow, *Pimephales promelas*) are available in every local fish store. They are cheap and are eagerly eaten by predatory fish. There may be times when you will have to use them to get a predator to eat, but I recommend that you avoid them whenever possible. Part of the reason is that they are raised, shipped, and housed in crowded conditions and may be riddled with diseases and parasites. These threats are more significant if you're feeding them to other freshwater fish, but some of these ailments can be transferred to marine fish as well, so why take the chance? Even more dangerous over time is the nutritional effect of feeder fish. Studies have shown that feeder goldfish may have fifteen or twenty times more saturated fats than the natural fish prey of a marine predator. Over time, these saturated fats will do the same thing to marine fish as too many potato chips will do to humans—make them obese, listless, and cause multiple organ malfunctions, especially fatty liver degeneration. If you have predators such as groupers, triggerfish, lionfish, and the like, please consider using glass shrimp or crawfish instead. These crustaceans will get just as active a feeding response from your predators, but with better nutrition and lower risk of parasites and disease.

Brine Shrimp

The lowly brine shrimp, usually referred to as *Artemia salina* (although many species are probably involved), are small crustaceans that reach a maximum of about a quarter-inch in length. If you're old enough, you probably remember the "Sea Monkeys" sold by mail-order ads in comic books. This was a clever marketing scheme to sell brine shrimp.

Brine shrimp inhabit salty ponds and lakes around the world, but most of the brine shrimp sold in North America are harvested from the Great Salt Lake in Utah and San Francisco Bay in California. They are available at your local fish store frozen, freeze-dried, and probably even live. Live brine shrimp are an excellent first food for small grazing fish, and even predators such as lionfish will often snap at them. Very tiny fish can be fed newly hatched brine shrimp, which are each about the size of a grain of salt and are also available frozen or as dried cysts (eggs) that you can hatch yourself.

The potential problem with brine shrimp is that they have very inconsistent nutritional value. The newly hatched brine shrimp (the larval stage called the nauplius—plural, nauplii) are typically relatively high in protein and essential fatty acids, but after that their nutritional value is largely dependent on what they have been eating—in the wild, mostly single-celled algae. In other words, the most nutri-

● Brine shrimp are most effective as a food source if you first soak live brine in a vitamin-mineral mixture before offering them to your fish. Alternatively, some commercial brands of frozen brine shrimp are vitamin supplemented.

● This feeding platter contains (clockwise from lower left) frozen algae-based food; a krill, prawn, and silverside mixture; a bloodworm and mysid shrimp blend, and a carnivore blend.

tional part of a brine shrimp is not the shrimp itself but what's in its gut. Unless they are very fresh, the live brine shrimp at your local fish store probably have empty guts and relatively low nutritional value. Additionally, the quality of brine shrimp varies from place to place and season to season. Frozen brine shrimp may be better in terms of nutrition, but sometimes it takes the motion of a live shrimp to get a stubborn fish to start feeding. When you see live brine shrimp for sale, try to buy those that are bright red in color rather than brown, as the red ones are more nutritious for your fish.

The nutritional value of brine shrimp can be improved by soaking them in a vitamin-mineral supplement (some frozen brands already have added vitamins) or by holding live brine shrimp for a few days and feeding them nutritional supplements before offering them to your fish. The bottom line, however, is that you shouldn't rely on brine shrimp—or any single food—to keep your fish healthy. Only a varied diet can accomplish that.

⬆ If you feed your fish live prey, glass shrimp are a healthier choice than goldfish. These shrimp are easy to gut-load for added nutritional value and their longevity in freshwater and marine tanks will keep your predatory fish on the hunt until every last one is caught.

Mysid Shrimp

Mysid shrimp are somewhat larger than brine shrimp, up to an average of one-half inch (1.2 cm) in length. They usually have a daily migrational pattern, feeding on the bottom by day and swimming to the surface at night to feed on small plankton, including other crustaceans. Although usually not available live at your local fish store, mysid shrimp are readily available frozen. The species usually available is the freshwater *Mysis relicta*. While their nutritional value, like that of brine shrimp, is somewhat dependent on what they have eaten, mysid shrimp usually contain more essential fatty acids (including the desirable omega-3 and omega-6 fatty acids). Another plus is that they often stimulate a more aggressive feeding response from grazing fish—I've seen butterflyfish that would only pick at brine shrimp go positively nuts over mysids!

Krill

Krill, usually *Euphausia superba*, are perhaps the most nutritious of the small crustaceans available. Although you can only get them in frozen or freeze-dried form, fish that eat crustaceans accept them with gusto. Krill can be up to 2 inches (5 cm) in length, but are sold at a variety of sizes down to as little as one-half inch (1.2 cm). To give you some idea of their nutritional value, consider the fact that baleen whales, including the massive blue whale (the largest animal on Earth), eat almost nothing else but these planktonic crustaceans. Frozen krill may be up to 15 percent protein (a very high "raw" percentage compared with most other foods) and high levels of omega fatty acids. When you remove the moisture from krill, as happens when they are freeze-dried, they may be more than 60 percent protein by dry weight! They also have lots of carotenoid pigments, which are important for maintaining the colors of red, orange, or yellow fish. The color of these fish will fade over time in captivity if they don't get carotenoids in their diet. Red brine shrimp are a good source, but pale in comparison (pun intended) to krill.

Glass Shrimp

About an inch in length, glass, grass, or ghost shrimp of the genus *Palaemonetes* and relatives are near-transparent shrimp that live in temperate and tropical estuaries worldwide. They can tolerate both full-fresh and full-marine water. In recent years they have become as widely available as feeder goldfish, and at a comparable price. If you have a predatory fish that refuses to eat nonliving food, glass shrimp are a far superior option to feeder goldfish or guppies. The

SNEAKY CRAWFISH

Be sure that you actually see the crawfish being eaten; if one gets away and dies in a hidden spot, it will pollute the water as it decomposes, potentially killing everything in the tank. (This same warning applies to any nonmarine creature used as a food for your fish.)

◉ Supervise your fish when you offer crawfish prey. These freshwater animals won't survive long in your marine tank, and a decomposing crawfish can quickly pollute the entire aquarium.

shrimp have moderate levels of essential fatty acids compared with krill or mysids, but it is easy to "gut-load" these crustaceans by feeding them nutritional supplements for several days before using them as food. An additional advantage of glass shrimp is that they will live indefinitely in your tank until they are eaten. You also shouldn't underestimate the value of the thrill of the chase to a predatory fish. Being able to stalk and capture prey in a natural manner, rather than just being "spoon-fed," is a valuable stress reducer for captive fish.

Crawfish

For fish too large to take glass shrimp, freshwater crawfish (usually *Procambarus clarkii* and *P. alleni* at your local fish store) are an option. These are basically freshwater lobsters, and, even though they will not survive long in a marine environment, they will live long enough to tempt a predatory fish into striking. Like glass shrimp, freshwater crawfish can be gut-loaded to increase their nutritional content.

Blackworms

Blackworms, *Lumbriculus* species, are small, freshwater annelid worms (annelids include the familiar garden earthworms) that are available live at your local fish store. Marine aquarists' opinion on blackworms is generally split down the middle. Some feel they should never be offered to marine fish, and others believe that they are a fine food in moderation. I agree with the latter. Blackworms sometimes get a bad rap by being superficially similar to tubifex worms, which are also freshwater annelids and notorious for being contaminated with sewage (and thus con-

⬆ A freshwater blackworm should live just long enough in your marine tank for a hungry fish to snatch it.

DISTINGUISHING LIVE WORMS FROM DEAD WORMS

It is important to make sure that blackworms are alive when fed; bacteria or toxins (or both) in dead worms can sicken or kill fish that eat them. Rinse a group of worms gently in a basin of cool water—any dead worms (which are grayish or white) will float away, and the live worms will clump together.

taminated with bacteria and pollutants). Blackworms are about 1.5 inches (3.8 cm) long and blackish in color; tubifex are much smaller and generally red in color. Blackworms are aquacultured, but tubifex are collected.

I am not aware of any detailed nutritional analysis of blackworms, but they likely have a good protein content. They quickly die when exposed to salt, but when placed in a marine tank they will twitch appetizingly for a few seconds, which is all you need for most small fish to respond to them. I'll stress that blackworms must be fed in small quantities—every last one must be consumed before it hits the bottom, or you risk polluting the water as they decompose.

● Gut-cleaned earthworms are a high-protein food treat for your marine fish.

Earthworms

They can be a little be tricky to use, but whole earthworms are a valuable food for larger fish and, when chopped, even for smaller fish. They may be available from the local fish store and definitely from bait dealers. The tricky part is getting rid of their gut contents. Unlike the crustaceans we discussed earlier, which you actually want to stuff with food before feeding them to your fish, earthworms need to be emptied because they eat soil, and you don't want that in your aquarium. To clean them, first remove them from the soil they

● Many small- to medium-sized fish are fond of bloodworms.

came in and place them in a container of damp moss. Over several days, they will clear their gut contents. To make sure, gently roll a pencil over the worm from just below the clitellum (the band near the head) to the tip of the tail. Any remaining soil should be forced out. Rinse the worm with fresh water and you are ready to go.

I really learned to appreciate earthworms as a potential food for large marine fish when I saw the reaction of a tame blue-spotted stingray (*Taeniura lymma*) that would eagerly swim up to be hand-fed when offered an earthworm treat. In moderation, and when carefully cleaned, they are a high-protein food that should not be overlooked.

Bloodworms and Glassworms

These are not actually worms at all but are the freshwater larvae of small midge insects. They are occasionally available live, particularly in the winter months, but they are always available frozen. They are definitely not a natural food, but many fish go for them. Damselfish, despite the fact that many species are herbivores in the wild, really go for bloodworms. So do many butterflyfish, wrasses, basslets, and a host of other small- to medium-sized fish. I would be cautious about using them in large quantities, but bloodworms and glassworms are foods no aquarist should be without.

Seafoods

Here I'm considering various crustaceans, mollusks, and fish available at your local fishmonger or the seafood section of your supermarket. Many of the sea creatures that would be delicacies at a human dinner table are just as worthy as food for your fish. Some of these are especially useful for getting a stubborn fish to feed. For example, the copperband butterflyfish, *Chelmon rostratus*, is often hesitant to start feeding in captivity (one of the reasons it's usually considered a fish for experienced aquarists) but will often be tempted by a fresh mussel on the half shell. Fish that prefer meaty foods also favor chunks of scallop. Squid, either strips of flesh or whole tentacles, is another favorite. Shrimp tails can be used, but I recommend soaking them in a nutritional supplement first. Small whole fish such as smelt or sardines (fresh or frozen only, not canned!) are far more nutritious than feeder goldfish for lionfish, morays, and groupers. Triggerfish or larger wrasses will enjoy chomping on some blue crab pieces, shell and all. None of these foods should be used exclusively, but don't overlook the fish market for widening your fish food choices.

Veggies

Fish such as surgeonfish (tangs) and pygmy angelfish are largely or even exclusively herbivorous. We've devoted a lot of space to predatory fish, but what about the vegetarians?

The best foods for these fish are what they eat in nature—algae. Specifically, most species prefer the leafy varieties, usually called "macroalgae" in aquarium literature. The green *Caulerpa* species are readily available at the local fish store; even better if you can get them are the red *Gracilaria* species, which are less commonly sold but are abundant if you happen to live along the coasts of North America. Some veggie-loving fish prefer filamentous ("hair") algae,

but I don't recommend deliberately introducing marine hair algae to your tank or it will probably overrun everything. You could try feeding some freshwater hair algae in small amounts, but be sure to remove any that is uneaten or it will decompose and could degrade water quality.

⬆ A clown triggerfish noshes on a lettuce treat.

In recent years, it has become common to find nori seaweed in supermarkets. This is the seaweed that is used to wrap sushi, and seaweeds (kelp, for example) are really large macroalgae. Make sure you get nori that has no added preservatives, spices, or the like. Your local fish store sells feeding clips with suction cups that are specifically intended for anchoring nori and other veggies so that grazing fish can work on them.

In addition to nori, you can find numerous other vegetable choices at the supermarket (get some for yourself while you're at it!). Leaf lettuce is readily accepted by many species, but I really don't recommend it, as it is somewhat lacking in nutritional value. Better leafy vegetables include kale, mustard greens, and spinach leaves, all of which should be briefly blanched in boiling water before using them as fish food. Blanching slightly softens the veggies and breaks down cell walls to make the food more digestible. Blanched peas are also a great supplement. You can also try blanched zucchini, which has long been a staple for keeping the freshwater "pleco" suckermouth catfish, but is surprisingly ignored by marine hobbyists.

Because vegetarian fish are grazers, it's important to have some vegetable matter available at all times for them to pick at. Simply replace it as it is consumed, or when the fish stop picking at it. An added benefit of all this grazing is that it tends to reduce aggression, especially with angels and tangs, which can be quarrelsome with conspecifics. It can sometimes happen that one fish hogs all the food and keeps the others away from it; more often, a group of grazing fish will spend so much time feeding that these fish will have less time to harass each other.

Frozen Prepared Foods

By "prepared" I mean foods with multiple ingredients that are blended with some special goal in mind. This distinguishes them from, say, frozen brine shrimp, which has a single ingredient and usually isn't very processed. For example, there are frozen prepared foods that contain sponges and are intended for large angelfish such as *Holacanthus* species, which require sponge flesh in their diets. Other prepared foods are vegetable-based for tangs. Others are specifically formulated for pickers such as butterflyfish. There are many, many varieties of prepared frozen foods, and they are a nutritional option you shouldn't ignore. Some provide foods items, such as the sponges, that can't easily be

🔁 Some prepared frozen food varieties have high protein content to supplement your fish's diet or other ingredients that you won't readily find elsewhere.

obtained elsewhere. The best advice I can give you is to read the ingredients carefully, know the species they're intended for, and do not use them to the complete exclusion of live and fresh foods.

Flake and Pellet Foods

Dried flake and pellet foods are usually based on fish meal and/or shrimp, but there are also vegetable-based varieties (usually using *Spirulina* algae). Depending on the quality of the ingredients, flake and pellet foods can be anywhere from excellent to marginal. The old saying that "you get what you pay for" is often true here—cheap varieties often have a lot of filler or low-quality (often oily) fish meal, and expensive varieties have more krill, shrimp, or other ingredients aside from the fish meal.

I really don't mean to slam flakes and pellets, as some of them are excellent. In particular, brands that are made specifically for color enhancing are indispensable for maintaining red coloration in flame angels, squirrelfish, and other red and/or orange fish. However, I consider flakes and pellets only supplementary. In most cases, I believe that live, fresh, and frozen foods should make up the bulk of the diet for your marine fish.

❶ Flake and pellet foods can be excellent nutrition sources—especially color-enhancing brands. I recommend, though, that you use these foods only as a supplement to your fish's total diet.

You must be careful when feeding flakes and pellets. Flake foods, in particular, are easy to overfeed because they fragment into tiny particles and drift about the tank. However, if you feed tiny portions, they can be useful for multiple daily feedings for damselfish and other small, hyperactive species. Pellet foods can give you somewhat better portion control because you can match the pellet size (most pellet foods are available in large and small sizes) to your fish and select a floating or sinking pellet based on the habits of your fish. Additionally, if you happen to overfeed with pellets, you can scoop out the excess with a fine-meshed net.

TANK MONITORING

If you've put into practice the tools and techniques covered in this book, you should have a sparkling marine aquarium with a thriving community of lovely fish. From here on out, regular maintenance is the key—including monitoring salinity, alkalinity, temperature, and nitrogen levels.

Salinity and Specific Gravity

Obviously, we need to measure the salinity of our aquarium water and make sure we have just the right amount of "salt." This is not as easy as you might think. Direct measurement of salinity is usually done with either a conductivity meter or a refractometer. We all know that electricity and water don't mix, but that's because of the dissolved solids in water, especially salts. Remember, these are charged atoms—ions—and ions conduct electricity very well. Distilled water, believe it or not, is a poor conductor of electricity. The more salt in the water, the better its electrical conductivity; a conductivity meter measures this and calculates the salinity. Seawater also conducts light differently than pure distilled water, so a refractometer measures the difference in light refraction between seawater and pure water and calculates the salinity. Unfortunately, conductivity meters and refractometers are expensive and delicate.

Fortunately, there is a workable way to measure salinity indirectly: specific gravity, which we touched on earlier. Once again, remember that seawater is heavier than distilled or freshwater. Specific gravity is a measure of how heavy a water sample is compared with pure water. Because the salts in seawater displace water, floating objects will float higher in seawater and lower in freshwater. For example, a boat will float higher in the water in the ocean than it will in a freshwater lake. Using this principle, it is possible to produce the hydrometer, a tapered glass float with markings to indicate the specific gravity of water. This indirectly indicates the salinity of the water. The advantage of hydrometers is that they are much less expensive than conductivity meters or refractometers.

Like all floating objects, a hydrometer will float lower in pure (fresh) water and higher in seawater. The specific gravity measurement is determined by where the water surface meets the stem of the hydrometer—but there's a trick to reading a hydrometer correctly. Because of surface tension, the water surface will actually rise slightly where it meets the stem of the hydrometer, forming a little cone of water called a meniscus. The correct hydrometer reading is at the bottom of this cone.

As mentioned in Chapter 1, most tropical, open-ocean water has a specific gravity of approximately 1.025 to 1.026. Many aquarists, however, advocate keeping a marine aquarium at a specific gravity slightly lower than that found in nature, or about 1.022 to 1.023.

Is specific gravity really that simple? Well, almost, but not exactly. A couple of things can throw off your readings. First, to get an accurate reading with a floating hydrometer, it needs to be in perfectly still water; in an aquarium it will probably bob up and down at least a little. You should also know that the glass hydrometers are usually calibrated to be accurate at 75°F (25°C). Like all other matter in the universe, seawater contracts when it is cold and expands when it is warm, so temperature changes the specific gravity; and if your aquarium is warmer or colder than 75°F, you will get a slightly inaccurate reading, although not so far off as to be dangerous to most marine life. To deal with these problems, a new generation of hydrometers is designed with a floating pointer; you just dip the unit into your aquarium and scoop a water sample, then place the device on a flat surface. The pointer will indicate the specific gravity. These newer hydrometers are also temperature-corrected to read more accurately at aquarium temperatures.

Hydrometer

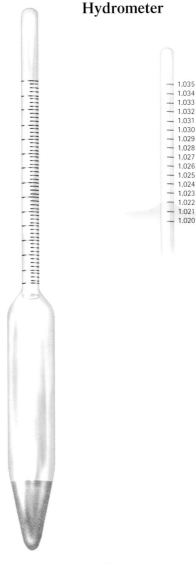

1.035
1.034
1.033
1.032
1.031
1.030
1.029
1.028
1.027
1.026
1.025
1.024
1.023
1.022
1.021
1.020

Alkalinity and pH

Alkalinity is really just alkaline buffering. Because marine fish and other organisms are adapted to an alkaline environment, we want to "encourage" the water to stay alkaline. Calcium, carbonates, bicarbonates, and hydroxides are among the chemicals that will act to keep alkaline water alkaline; think of them as acid sponges. If there is a slight imbalance of the alkaline chemicals, they will be able to keep up with the acids produced by biological processes and keep your aquarium water on the safe, alkaline side. However, because the acids are continually being produced, the alkaline chemicals can get "used up" if they are not replenished. There are commercial products sold to help restore the alkalinity in a marine aquarium, and even household baking soda (sodium bicarbonate) will raise pH. However, in most cases it should only be necessary to use these buffering agents in reef aquariums because of the truly massive amount of life they contain. In our tank that is fish-only or nearly so, regular water changes will do fine to maintain enough alkalinity to buffer the water to between 8.0 and 8.4. The type of substrate (sand or gravel) in your aquarium can also be selected to help buffer the pH (as discussed in Chapter 2). If the pH quickly drops below 8.0, it generally means that the tank is overstocked, you are overfeeding and the excess food is rotting, or something has died—or all of the above.

Temperature

We've already mentioned how temperature variations affect specific gravity, but temperature has other effects, too. Temperature varies tremendously in the world's oceans, from at or near freezing (32°F or 0°C) in polar seas to 80°F (27°C) or more in the tropics. The optimum temperature for your home marine aquarium will depend on the species you wish to keep and where they originated. But, if you intend to keep coral reef fish, an optimum temperature would be 74°F to 78°F (23°C to 26°C). All of the fish species we are considering in this book can be kept within this temperature range; however, it would be better to aim for the lower end of this range because warmer seawater holds less dissolved oxygen than cooler water.

Lower temperatures also reduce the metabolic rates of your fish because they are "cold-blooded." With lower metabolic rates, they will excrete less waste and have a lower, slower impact on filtration, alkalinity, etc. They will also eat slightly less and stretch your food budget. Even a few degrees in temperature can have a powerful effect on fish metabolism: a ten-degree Fahrenheit (twelve-degree Celsius) temperature increase may double the metabolic rate of a fish! Please don't reduce the temperature too much, however, because fish are adapted for a particular temperature range on the basis of their geographic origin, and you don't want to push them outside their comfort zone. To do so risks stressing or even killing them.

OXYGENATION

If you have sufficient filtration and aeration, the oxygen difference between 74°F and 78°F is unlikely to spell the difference between life and death for your fish. Yet, every little advantage you can get gives you greater leeway for error if problems arise. Since gas exchange (oxygen in and carbon dioxide out) occurs primarily at the water's surface, it is important to create turbulence at the surface with streams of water or bubbles. Most filters have aerating features that make this easy.

Nitrogen Cycle

A marine aquarium that is newly set up is essentially sterile. There are no colonies of the nitrifying bacteria that drive the nitrogen cycle. If fish and/or invertebrates are now added to the tank, the nitrogen cycle will begin. As the animals eat and excrete, the ammonium levels will increase. The animals carry small numbers of nitrifying bacteria with them, and the bacteria will colonize the tank and slowly begin to convert the ammonium to nitrite and the nitrite to nitrate. As you monitor the levels with your test kits, you will see the ammonium level peak and then drop off to near zero as the bacteria get a handle on it; then you will see the nitrite level increase, peak at a lower maximum than the ammonium, and also drop back to near zero; finally, the nitrate levels will build slowly but steadily. Algae use the nitrates as fertilizer, but you will also need to dilute them by doing regular water changes.

Unfortunately, during the cycling process, the ammonia and nitrite will peak at levels well above those that are lethal to most fish and invertebrates. Therefore, you need to first establish bacterial colonies before adding any delicate animals. The use of live rock and live sand (as discussed in Chapter 2) will introduce ready-to-go colonies of live nitrifying bacteria to your aquarium, perhaps enough to prevent dangerously high levels of ammonium or nitrite from developing, but almost certainly reducing the length of time toxic levels exist. Alternatively, a handful of dirty gravel from an established tank, or a pint or two of water siphoned from a filter on an established tank, can serve as a source of nitrifying bacteria.

Long story short, it is hard to say how long it will take a tank to cycle completely. It may be anywhere from a few days to a few weeks, depending on how effectively you can front-load the tank with nitrifying bacteria. Traditionally, aquarists have used hardy fish such as damselfish to cycle a tank, but this is not foolproof. If the damsels survive (and they don't always make it), you might be left with the problem of what to do with them; they're aggressive and probably not what you want in your display fish. I have often used the black molly (*Poecilia sphenops*) instead. Mollies are usually sold as freshwater fish, but if you acclimate them over the course of four to six hours, they will adapt to seawater. They are a good source of ammonium to culture your bacteria, are cheaper than damsels, and, in my experience, can survive the high ammonia and nitrite spikes.

CHAPTER 4

Ideal Fish for Your Marine Aquarium

These following sections include fish that I consider ideal for a beginning marine hobbyist. In general, I have tried to select species on the basis of availability (usually easy to find in your local fish store) and "keepability" (easy to feed, relatively disease resistant). Additionally, the majority of the fish I will talk about are moderately priced, as marine fish go; most of them are in the range of $20 to $50.

A few are more expensive but are included for hobbyists with more expensive tastes. Otherwise, I have tried to include a broad range of fish—large and small, peaceful and aggressive, and so on—with the hope that all readers of this book will find something to their liking. More experienced readers will probably disagree with me on some of the species I'm including, as well as on those I'm leaving out. To be sure, there are hundreds more fish species that you could see in your local fish store than we will consider here (I am leaving out whole families, in some cases), and some of them are worthy specimens for your aquarium. My intention is to provide you with some good examples, but not the only ones.

MORAY EELS

Moray eels—like sharks, squids and octopuses, and a few other marine creatures—have a near-legendary status and are known even to folks who know almost nothing else about marine life. Unfortunately, much of what people think they know about these "monsters of the deep" is extremely inaccurate.

The more than 200 species of moray eels compose the family Muraenidae. These snake-like eels lack scales and paired fins, and the dorsal fin is continuous with the tail and anal fin. Morays are found worldwide in temperate and tropical seas, and a few are found in brackish or even freshwater habitats. Depending on species, adult size may be less than 12 inches (30 cm) to more than 12 feet (3.7 m)! Moray eels are almost always associated with hard substrates—rocky or coral reefs that provide them with caves and crevices. All species are predaceous, but some species feed primarily on fish, other species prefer soft-bodied invertebrates such as octopuses and squids, and others are specialized to crush the hard shells of crustaceans, snails, and clams.

Morays have an undeserved reputation for viciousness. Part of this is probably because of their appearance, evoking the same knee-jerk phobia some people have to snakes (and don't get me started on that, because I like snakes, too). Morays also open their mouths wide when they breathe, which may look like a threatening display of their pointed teeth. However, morays in general are no more vicious than any other predatory fish. Although it is true that some of the large species can be dangerous to divers, there are only a few records of truly unprovoked attacks. Most morays are shy cave dwellers that retreat from humans—and when they bite, it is almost always in defense or because they have been fed by humans and expect a handout. Feeding wild morays is a bad idea, just as it is with bears or any other wild animals.

Moray eels are popular with aquarists who like big, mean fish (or at least fish with a mean reputation). Unfortunately, because the majority of moray species are 4 to 6 feet (1.2 to 1.8 m) in length as adults and can be predaceous with tankmates, morays are beyond the capabilities of most home aquarists. However, there are a few species that do well in the home aquarium that I can recommend. Two species, the zebra moray and the snowflake moray, are especially common in the aquarium trade, but several dozen other species may be available from time to time. In general, I would avoid species that have strongly hooked jaws (for example, species of the genus *Enchelycore* such as the dragon moray, *E. pardalis*). These species are fish-eaters and should be kept alone; they may even attack other morays, including conspecifics.

For aquarists who want to keep a moray eel, here are a few guidelines: Aquascaping for morays should include a variety of caves and overhangs that create shade spots, as morays are primarily nocturnal and do not like bright light. The caves should be big enough that the eel can fit its entire body inside. It is also important that the caves are sturdy! Rocks and artificial corals that are loosely stacked can easily collapse as the moray moves around, perhaps crushing the eel and even cracking the aquarium and creating a disaster. You can use aquarium silicone to cement rocks and corals into a safe structure before placing it in the aquarium; if you are using live rock, there are aquarium-safe putty cements available that can be used underwater.

Another very important consideration is a heavy, very tight-fitting tank cover. Morays are escape artists and can push up a loose-fitting lid or slither out of filter access holes or other small gaps in the cover. This is probably a by-product of their feeding habits—morays will probe any hole or space for something edible, usually at night. Many aquarists have made the unpleasant discovery of a dried moray on the carpet in the morning; I'll admit that I learned the hard way that you can't underestimate the Houdiniesque ability of morays!

Tankmates should be selected with care. Even morays that are not specialized fish eaters may eat a tankmate if it is small enough or conveniently shaped (such as cylindrical). In addition, tankmates should have compatible activity patterns. Morays tend to be disturbed by fast-moving fish such as snappers, large tangs such as unicornfish (*Naso*), and large wrasses. More ideal tankmates include other retiring or slow-moving species; many aquarists have successfully kept morays with lionfish, medium-sized groupers, and large angelfish. Except for the fish-eating species, most morays may also be kept with other morays of similar size, including conspecifics and eels of other species, as long as there are sufficient hiding places for all.

Because morays have poor eyesight and because they may lose out to more competitive tankmates (including other morays) at feeding time, the eels should be individually fed with long tongs. Waving the food item in front of the eel or even gently poking it in the snout will usually get a feeding response. Most morays will feed with gusto once they are acclimated to aquarium life, but their eagerness to eat can actually be a problem—morays can easily become obese in captivity. Keep in mind that a moray generally spends most of its time hanging out in its cave and not using a lot of energy. A moray will do well on only two to three feedings per week of meaty foods such as whole shrimp, pieces of crab with legs still attached, chunks of clam or scallop, and pieces of squid.

🔽 The chainlink eel (*Echidna catenata*) will grow to about 28 inches (71cm) and need at least a 30-gallon (114-L) tank.

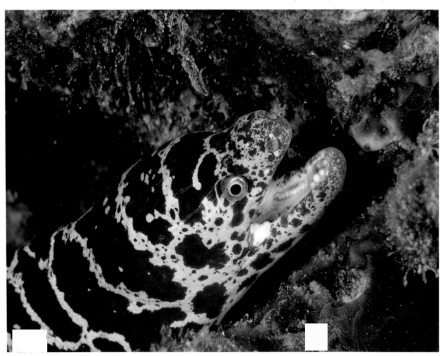

⭐ **ZEBRA MORAY**

Gymnomuraena zebra
Geographic Range: Indo-Pacific
Adult Size: 36 inches (91 cm)
Temperament: Peaceful with conspecifics and with other species
Food: Live crustaceans; chunks of shrimp, crab, clam, scallop, and squid

Zebra Moray

The zebra moray is one of the more manageable species of moray eels. Although it is not a small fish, a 3-foot (91-cm) adult moray is not as big as it sounds, particularly because it is not an active swimmer and will spend a lot of time tucked into a cave with just its head showing. As with most morays, it is nocturnal by nature, but zebra morays will become acclimated to daytime activity in the aquarium and, although they will still prefer the shadows, they will not be invisible inhabitants of your tank.

Zebra morays have molariform (molar-like) teeth, which are used to crush their typical prey—crustaceans and mollusks. So, although you can't trust them with your crabs, shrimp, or snails, their having molariform teeth is good news when it comes to keeping a zebra moray in a fish-only aquarium—because these eels almost never prey on fish and can be trusted with all but the smallest specimens. These morays are placid, sedate animals that basically live and let live.

Zebra morays are usually seen at your local fish store at sizes of approximately 18 to 24 inches (46 to 61 cm). Within this size range they can be kept in aquariums as small as 40 gallons (151 L). But, to allow for growth and the addition of a few tankmates, I recommend a minimum tank size of 75 gallons (284 L). Zebra morays get along well with conspecifics and with other nonaggressive moray species. When kept together, two or three zebra morays may even choose to cohabit in a large cave and make a spectacular display when they do, but you should provide enough hiding places that they can have individual crevices if they prefer.

Because of their unusually placid natures, zebra morays may require some patience on your part to get them acclimated to aquarium life. A zebra moray may settle in more quickly if it is the first animal placed in the aquarium (meaning that it has no competition), although it's not absolutely necessary to do this. You may also have to offer some live food to get it feeding, such as live glass shrimp (which are brackish or marine and will live indefinitely in your tank) or even a freshwater crawfish or two (which will live for a few minutes in saltwater, long enough to be eaten). If you gradually switch over to offering shrimp tails or blue crab legs from feeding tongs, you'll be home free. After that, you can offer almost any meaty food and the eel will accept it.

 SNOWFLAKE MORAY

Echidna nebulosa

Geographic Range: Indo-Pacific

Adult Size: up to 30 inches (75 cm)

Temperament: occasionally aggressive toward conspecifics; sometimes overzealous eaters

Food: live crustaceans; chunks of shrimp, crab, clam, scallop, and squid

Snowflake Moray

The snowflake moray is another excellent moray for the aquarium. It is slightly smaller than the zebra moray and somewhat less shy. Although it will eat fish small enough to swallow, it is generally peaceful and in most cases will be a nonaggressive member of a community fish-only aquarium; however, like the zebra moray, the snowflake moray is primarily a crustacean predator and cannot be kept with shrimp, crabs, and lobsters.

The only exception regarding this eel's generally peaceful behavior is that it can get overly eager at feeding time and might bite a tankmate in a feeding frenzy. Try to feed the eel(s) first, individually with tongs, before you feed other tankmates. Even so, be prepared to gently shoo away the eel with the tongs if it comes out and behaves rambunctiously when you're feeding the other fish. The bright side of this strong feeding reaction is that snowflake morays usually adjust to aquarium life and feeding schedules more quickly than zebra morays.

Snowflakes are available in a wide variety of sizes, from juveniles only 8 or 10 inches (20 to 25 cm) long to young adults of 24 inches (61 cm) or more. Although all should do well in the home aquarium, as with many species the most adaptable seem to be those in the medium size range, about 12 to 18 inches (30 to 46 cm).

Snowflake morays get along very well with other moray species of a similar size, and they make a very nice display when kept with zebra morays. They also usually get along well with other snowflakes, although occasional individuals will attack another snowflake. Whether this behavior is territorial, sexual, or just plain perversity is unknown. Therefore, if you wish to keep more than one snowflake moray in the same tank, it is best to introduce them at the same time so that no individual has a territorial advantage.

SQUIRRELFISH AND SOLDIERFISH

There are more than sixty species in the family Holocentridae, commonly known as squirrelfish (subfamily Holocentrinae) and soldierfish (subfamily Myripristinae). Holocentrids are found worldwide on coral and rocky reefs in tropical seas, with a few species extending into temperate waters. They are universally nocturnal fish; although, like most nocturnal species, they will get used to being somewhat active by day in an aquarium.

Almost all squirrelfish and soldierfish species are red in color. Squirrelfish are often striped with alternating bands of red and white and have a relatively long snout, whereas soldierfish are usually solid red on the body and have a blunt snout and very large eyes. (They are usually sold as "bigeye squirrelfish" in the fish trade.) You might think that being red would make these fish extremely conspicuous on the reef. But, because red light does not penetrate very far in the water column, in deeper water or at night the dim light is bluish; so, in this reduced lighting a red fish actually looks black. Thus, red is the perfect color for a nocturnal or deep-water fish; in fact, many of the weird deep-sea fish trawled up by biologists are red.

On the reef, squirrelfish and soldierfish spend their days in crevices or in the shadows under large outcroppings of plate corals, in schools sometimes numbering in the hundreds, packed close together. At night they emerge from their hiding places like bats leaving a cave, fanning out over the reef but still staying in schools. They hunt for small crustaceans, worms, and other small invertebrates, and sometimes for small fish, too.

An interesting feature of squirrelfish is that they are vocal—they use grunts and clicks to communicate with each other. This helps to keep a school organized in the darkness and may also be used to help an individual claim "personal space" within a school, although most species are not strongly territorial.

In my humble opinion, squirrelfish and soldierfish are some of the most underrated fish with marine aquarium potential. The species in the family Holocentridae are attractive, hardy, resistant to disease, tolerant even of poor water quality, peaceful with other fish too large to swallow, and eat a wide variety of foods.

We should also be more appreciative of fish that can be kept with conspecifics. One of the biggest problems with many species of marine fish is conspecific aggression—put simply, it's hard to keep more than one per species per tank, and sometimes it's even hard to keep related species together. Unless you are lucky enough to purchase a mated pair, this is true of most angelfish, butterflyfish, groupers, basslets, and a host of other popular aquarium fish. However, this is not generally true of squirrelfish and soldierfish, and if you have a large tank (100 gallons [378 L] and up), keeping several or more conspecific holocentrids can be very attractive.

About the only specific requirement for keeping holocentrids is that they must be provided with shaded ledges, overhangs, and caves. Large shelves of artificial table or plate corals (*Acropora cytherea*, *A. hyacinthus*, and similar species) are ideal. The holocentrids will hang underneath them and will feel secure, but they will still be visible to you. With time, they will grow secure in the aquarium and will even make short forays out into the light, especially at feeding time.

Holocentrids are good tankmates with most fish as long as the tankmates do not compete with them for cave space. For example, moray eels would be a poor choice to house with these fish. Both squirrelfish and soldierfish would likely come out on the short end of it because they are easily driven from their caves by competitive species. Forced to dwell out in the open, the passive holocentrids will quickly become stressed, stop feeding, and eventually die if the situation is not remedied.

Squirrelfish and soldierfish will eat virtually any meaty foods you care to offer, including all prepared frozen foods and dried foods such as flakes and pellets. However, a diet rich in carotenoid pigments is important, or over time your holocentrids will fade from bright red to pale pink. Crustaceans are an excellent source of carotenoids and a natural prey item, so feed plenty of brine shrimp (live or frozen), krill (dried or frozen), and any frozen or pelleted prepared foods that are formulated to enhance red color in fish.

Longspine Squirrelfish

The longspine squirrelfish is one of several species commonly seen in your local fish store and is named for the long preopercular spine (visible on the lower part of the gill cover or operculum). In reality, I have seen several species sold under this name that were not the "real deal," including the very similar squirrelfish *H. ascensionis*, a more widespread species that also occurs in the Eastern Atlantic, the Gulf of Mexico, and northward in the Western Atlantic to at least New York. (I personally saw one a friend of mine collected when I was living in New Jersey.) Determining the exact species of an individual squirrelfish can be difficult because they are all red fish that are basically similar in appearance.

Regardless of species, however, all *Holocentrus* are identical in their captive care. Although they are often available as small as 3 to 4 inches (7.6 to 10.2 cm), they will grow into large specimens that need a lot of room; you should place them in an aquarium no smaller than 100 gallons (376 L) or at least have the capability to move them to an aquarium of that size as they grow. Longspine squirrelfish

 LONGSPINE SQUIRRELFISH

Holocentrus rufus

Geographic Range: Southwestern Atlantic; Caribbean

Adult Size: 12 inches (30 cm)

Temperament: peaceful with fish of similar size or larger but may consume smaller tankmates; does not exhibit conspecific aggression

Food: meaty foods (frozen or fresh) such as krill, shrimp, chopped scallop, and squid; most pelleted prepared diets

(and, indeed, most all squirrelfish of the genera *Holocentrus, Sargocentron,* and *Neoniphon*) are peaceful and inoffensive with all fish tankmates, except fish small enough to swallow. However, they will happily munch on shrimp, crabs, and a number of other invertebrates, so they should be restricted to fish-only tanks.

Blackbar Soldierfish

The blackbar soldierfish, named for the dark bar just behind the operculum, is the only *Myripristis* found in the Atlantic; the rest of the dozen or so species of the genus are Indo-Pacific in distribution and are only occasionally seen in the marine aquarium hobby. On the other hand, the blackbar soldierfish is a commonly available and reasonably priced fish that makes an excellent aquarium specimen. Though it is a moderately large aquarium fish at 8 inches (20 cm), it is smaller than the commonly available Atlantic squirrelfish.

 BLACKBAR SOLDIERFISH

Myripristis jacobus

Geographic Range: Eastern and Western Atlantic; Gulf of Mexico; Caribbean

Adult Size: 8 inches (20 cm)

Temperament: highly social but very light-shy; nonaggressive toward similar-sized tankmates

Food: mysid and brine shrimp, krill, bloodworms, all chopped meaty foods

Like the squirrelfish, the blackbar soldierfish is nocturnal and with its huge eyes is even more "light shy" than the squirrels. Deep, dark caves and overhangs are absolutely essential, and subdued lighting is recommended. In a more brightly lit aquarium, *M. jacobus* will stake out a favorite spot under an overhang but will streak out to grab food. You will notice that the mouths of soldierfish are sharply upturned, and this is an adaptation for taking small crustaceans from midwater. Unlike squirrelfish, which usually take food at any level in the aquarium, soldierfish usually will not feed off the bottom, so it is essential to make sure that they can see food as it sinks. Ideal foods include mysid shrimp, krill, brine shrimp, and bloodworms. Live brine shrimp or live guppies or mollies will tempt a newly acclimated specimen if it is reluctant to feed; however, once soldierfish start feeding, they rarely stop and will accept almost anything offered.

All soldierfish are highly social, perhaps even more so than squirrelfish. Although it takes a large aquarium (75 to 100 gallons [284 to 379 L] and larger) to house more than a couple soldierfish, it is worth the effort. They can also be kept singly and do not appear to be stressed by the lack of company. Virtually all nonaggressive fish species of a similar size will make good tankmates.

LIONFISH

The venomous scorpionfish (family Scorpaenidae) are found worldwide in temperate to tropical waters. The family includes nearly 400 species, such as the stonefish, some of the deadliest fish known; the rockfish, sold in seafood shops and restaurants as "ocean perch;" and the spectacular lionfish that are popular with aquarists.

Lionfish compose the subfamily Pteroinae, with two genera—*Pterois* and *Dendrochirus*—and a total of some sixteen currently recognized species. Almost all of these species make it into the hobby occasionally, but only five or six are seen with any regularity. All lionfish originate from the Indian and Pacific oceans; there are, for example, no native Atlantic lionfish.

Lionfish are brightly colored, usually striped fish with long, feather-like dorsal and pectoral fins, large heads, and big eyes. They are slow moving and often cruise boldly in midwater (especially the *Pterois* species) as if immune to attack. With few exceptions, they are. The "feathers" of the first dorsal fin are actually highly venomous spines, and the other fish that share the reef with lions seem to instinctively know to avoid them. Smaller, shorter venomous spines are located on the pelvic and anal fins. Each spine is hollow, like a hypodermic needle, and is connected at its base to a venom gland. A fleshy sheath covers the spine. When a lionfish is threatened, it raises its dorsal spines and tilts its head down to face the attacker spines-first. If the attacker does not back down, the lionfish will jab with its spines; if a spine makes contact, the fleshy sheath is pushed down and muscles contract the venom gland to inject its contents through the hollow spine. The venom causes intense pain and, when spined, even the most stubborn attacker will flee.

In their natural habitat, lionfish are top predators that prey on smaller fish and crustaceans. As conspicuous as they are when in cruise mode, lionfish can be surprisingly stealthy when feeding. The stubbier *Dendrochirus* species simply wait quietly on the bottom for an unwary fish or shrimp to approach within striking distance. On the other hand, *Pterois* species use gorgonians, feather stars, and other wavy creatures as cover from which to slowly stalk their prey (like a lion—get it?).

Although they're beautiful, you might ask why anyone would want to keep a predatory, venomous fish. Well, there is that danger factor—the same thing that encourages some people to keep venomous snakes and other dangerous animals. I don't stand here to pass judgment on that, one way or the other; however, I have kept lionfish on several occasions and can tell you an even more powerful factor contributing to their popularity: they have personality! People who keep them will tell you that they quickly become tame and will respond to their owners, beg for food, and generally behave like true pets. Lionfish also seem to be unusually perceptive as fish go. I once had a volitans lionfish that would come to the front of the tank and swim about actively whenever I came close, apparently begging for food, but would hide whenever anyone else came near that tank. It was obvious that the fish recognized me and could distinguish between me and all other humans who approached the tank. This at least confirms that lionfish have excellent eyesight, but it is also a behavior that tends to make you start thinking of the fish as a real pet with an individual personality.

So, lionfish are personable and indeed do become tame, but you should never forget that they are very dangerous. Although I was unable to locate even a single documented human fatality from a lionfish sting, there is no doubt that it is a very painful experience and conceivably could be life-threatening to a child, an elderly person, or someone with a medical condition. If you decide to keep a lionfish, you must do everything you can to avoid being stung, as well as know what to do if you are stung.

You should be aware that lionfish, like many marine fish, are territorial. When you stick your hand into the tank, perhaps to scrape some stubborn algae, even a "tame" lionfish may see it as a threat. Do not assume that even the most personable lionfish is domesticated. It is not a dog! Therefore, do not place your hand in the tank unless absolutely necessary; use tools such as long-handled algae scrapers. If you absolutely must place your hand in the tank, the lionfish must be confined. A temporary tank divider (available at your local fish store) can be used to keep the lionfish confined to a portion of the tank in which you are not working. And never, ever, place your hand in a tank unless you can see the lionfish; many people have been stung while reaching behind a piece of coral because they were sure the fish was at the other end of the tank (even though they couldn't see it!). Additionally, be very careful when netting or transferring lionfish.

If you are unlucky enough to be stung, you will probably be stung on the hand. The amount of venom injected will vary depending on the size of the fish and the number of spines that make contact, but you will experience searing pain up to at least the elbow, if not the

shoulder. Immediately have someone call for medical assistance, and then place the stung area into a container of hot but not scalding water—110°F to 115°F (43°C to 46°C). The venom is protein-based, and the hot water begins to denature (break down) the protein, which also reduces the pain. The pain should subside within twenty-four hours, although some patients report tingling or tenderness of the affected area for days or even weeks.

Okay, enough with the horror stories! As long as you stay safe, the captive care of lionfish is uneventful. They are very resistant to disease, forgiving of moderate variations in water quality, and surprisingly peaceful with fish they cannot swallow—but don't underestimate their big mouths. Additionally, lionfish can usually be kept with conspecifics or with other lionfish species without aggression problems, although you should watch their interactions closely at first, just to be sure.

Feeding lionfish is both easy and hard. What do I mean by that? Well, feeding them is easy because lionfish will greedily consume feeder goldfish or guppies, and have even been known to eat themselves to death from stomach rupture. However, feeder fish cannot be recommended as an exclusive diet, partly because of the risk of transferring diseases or parasites, and partly because they are not nutritional-

➊ This slow-moving red volitans lionfish cruises through its tank. If you choose to keep these predatory fish, you'll need at least a 55-gallon (208-L) tank to provide enough swimming room to prevent accidental spining of tankmates.

Dendrochirus zebra

Geographic Range: Indian Ocean, Western Pacific

Adult Size: 8 inches (20 cm)

Temperament: light-shy, males are somewhat aggressive toward conspecifics; will eat all smaller tankmates but are peaceful with fish the same size or larger

Food: live crustaceans; with patience, can be trained to take chunks of meaty food from tongs

ly complete. In the wild, lionfish also eat a lot of crustaceans, so supplementing the diet with gut-loaded grass shrimp or even the occasional freshwater crawfish is a good idea. Frozen or freeze-dried shrimp and krill are also nutritious, but it can be difficult to get a lionfish to take nonliving prey. Offering food at the end of long feeding tongs (safety first!) may work, but it takes patience. Another method that has worked well for me, at least with *Pterois*, is to make sure the fish is actively "begging" and then to throw several thawed frozen shrimp into the tank so that they really smack the water surface. This motion (and maybe the sound) usually triggers the lion to snap at the food. Fortunately, after a little bit of training, lions become accustomed to taking nonliving food, although more patience is required with *Dendrochirus* than with *Pterois*. Small lionfish should be fed every day, but larger specimens need to be fed only every other day and perhaps even only every third day. Like many larger marine fish, they are prone to obesity in captivity unless you carefully control their intake.

Dwarf Lionfish

The dwarf lionfish, like other members of the genus *Dendrochirus*, is a stubbier-looking fish compared with the more regal *Pterois*. Please don't think that means they are unattractive! In fact, the dwarf lionfish is very beautiful, especially when swimming with its pectoral fins outstretched. Unlike *Pterois* species, in which the pectoral rays are featherlike, a membrane joins the pectoral rays of *Dendrochirus* species, giving the pectorals a winglike appearance.

All of the *Dendrochirus* lionfish tend to be somewhat light-shy and retiring. They are fond of staking out a large cave and perching there for hours on end, sometimes upside down, and emerging at night to feed. However, like most of the nocturnal fish we've discussed, dwarf lionfish will become acclimated to daytime feeding and activity, though they usually will return to their caves after short jaunts in the open. Just make sure that their tank has an adequate number of caves and crevices, similar to what you might set up for squirrelfish. Because they are not very active, even a fair-sized individual (5 to 6 inches [12.7 to 15.2 cm]) can be kept in an aquarium as small as 30 gallons (114 L) if the tank is not overstocked.

Like other lionfish, the dwarf lionfish can be kept in conspecific groups, but not always without aggression. Males, which tend to be larger than females and have larger heads in proportion to the body, will usually chase other males. One male can be kept with multiple females; or groups of females and/or juveniles can be kept together. The problem is that you may not be able to sex them with certainty when you purchase them because they are usually seen for sale at about half their adult size; the differences in body and head size are usually obvious only with full-grown adults. If you keep this species in groups, observe their behavior carefully for signs of aggression and be prepared to move a harassed specimen (or its attacker) to another tank.

In my experience, the dwarf lionfish is more difficult to switch over to nonliving prey items than larger, more active lionfish such as *P. volitans*. Be patient, but also be prepared to spend some money on feeder fish, shrimp, and crawfish.

Volitans Lionfish

The volitans lionfish is undoubtedly one of the most recognizable marine fish. Even nonaquarists often know this fish and even know that it is venomous. It is frequently sold at a size of about 4 to 5 inches (10.2 to 15.2 cm), but this is a potentially large fish and should be kept in a tank no smaller than 55 to 75 gallons (208.2 to 284 L). Additionally, it is perhaps the most active of the lionfish and needs a great deal of open swimming room. Volitans lionfish will sometimes rest on a coral head, but you can keep the aquascaping to a minimum because they will spend far more of their time cruising regally through the open water. When given the space it needs, however, this is one of the most spectacular fish you can keep. I've already mentioned their engaging personalities.

Volitans lionfish primarily consume fish, and they are capable of consuming fish nearly their own size, so choose tankmates carefully. Additionally, although they rarely attack nonprey fish, accidental spining of a tankmate can happen if the tank is too small and/or crowded for the tankmates to get out of a lionfish's way.

⭐ VOLITANS LIONFISH

Pterois volitans

Geographic Range:
Indo-Pacific; Western
Atlantic (introduced)

Adult Size: 16 inches
(40 cm)

Temperament: greedy
eaters, aggressive and
predatory; peaceful
with larger fishes, but
will defend themselves
with venomous spines
if attacked

Food: live crustaceans;
can be trained to take
pieces of krill or
shrimp

Volitans lionfish are exceptionally greedy eaters, and many hobbyists stuff them nearly to bursting with feeder goldfish. As we have previously discussed, feeder goldfish are not recommended as a staple diet for anything. There may be times when you have to use them just to get predatory specimens such as lionfish eating regularly in captivity, but you should try hard to wean them off the goldfish as soon as possible. I've found that it is not difficult to get volitans lionfish started on nonliving by using the methods described above. Large shrimp, krill, and thawed frozen smelt are good nonliving foods to try, but I recommend soaking these in a vitamin and mineral supplement before feeding. Oddly enough, volitans lionfish can be susceptible to head-and-lateral-line-erosion (HLLE), a condition probably related to poor nutrition and more often seen in vegetarian fish such as tangs.

I should mention some of the confusion surrounding the identity of this fish. There are at least two distinct species seen in the hobby trade—the "black volitans" and the "red volitans," but at least four scientific names have been applied to them: *P. volitans*, of course, but also *P. lunulata*, *P. miles*, and *P. russelli*. The fish sold as the black volitans is, with few exceptions, the true *P. volitans*. Some ichthyologists consider the specimens from the Red Sea and Western Indian Ocean a separate species—*P. miles*—while other ichthyologists consider this merely a variety of *P. volitans*. However, the majority of black volitans in the hobby trade come from outside the range of *P. miles*; thus, most of them really are *P. volitans*.

The red volitans is another matter. When you see them in your local fish store, often mixed with *P. volitans*, you will notice that they have maroon-colored bands and shorter supraorbital tentacles. This is Russell's lionfish, *P. russelli*, but you'll never see it called that. Russell's lionfish is a little smaller than the true *P. volitans*—a maximum of about 12 inches (30.4 cm), but otherwise identical in behavior and care. Some books have referred to the red volitans as *P. lunulata*, but this is a species from Japanese waters and rarely, if ever, enters the aquarium trade.

I'd like to mention an odd tidbit of information about the volitans lionfish. In the past few years, this Indo-Pacific species has been showing up along the Atlantic coast of the United States, mostly the Carolinas, but also as far south as Florida and as far north as New York. No one is quite sure how they got there, but government scientists and officials were quick to blame aquarium hobbyists for accidental or intentional releases, even though there is not a shred of proof. (Many hobbyists and some scientists who are not on the government payroll consider it far more likely that larval lionfish hitched a ride in the ballast water of transoceanic ships; but, admittedly, there is no evidence of that either.) Regardless of how *P. volitans* invaded the Atlantic, it seems to be here to stay, and the ecological damage it could do as a non-native top predator remains to be seen.

I bring this up to make an important point: hobbyists must never, ever, release fish from their aquariums into the wild. The damage that an introduced species could do to a habitat where it has no natural enemies could be massive. In addition, doing so draws unwanted attention to our hobby from the government and lawmakers, and could lead to efforts to restrict or even outlaw our hobby. You must be a responsible aquarist, and part of that means that you must make a personal commitment to keep any fish you buy for its entire life. This also means that you have to do your homework and make sure that any fish you buy won't outgrow the largest tank you can provide for it. If we fail to educate ourselves and our fellow hobbyists to behave in a responsible manner, we endanger both natural habitats and the future of our hobby.

GROUPERS AND THEIR KIN

I am now going to lump together a pretty huge group of fish: the groupers, sea bass, basslets, and dottybacks. Together with several related groups, these form the massive family Serranidae, which comprises five families and approximately 450 species. To cover these fish in detail would require a book or more, so I'm going to cover just a few members of the family that have aquarium potential.

Many of these fish, especially those of the subfamily Epinephelinae, commonly called "groupers," are large—some *huge*! These fish are among the reef's top predators, and sharks are their

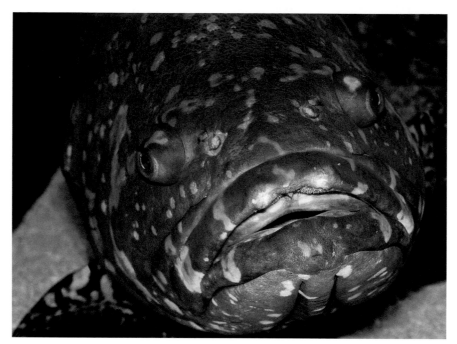

Though it has a beautiful pattern, this bumblebee grouper is not a reasonable choice for a typical home aquarium. You may find a small youngster at a fish store, but know that those of this species can grow up to 8 feet (244 cm) long!

only really serious competition. They are skillful predators on smaller fish and have perfected the ambush attack. Obviously, only the smallest of these animals are suited to the home aquarium, but it pays for the aquarist to be aware of even the giant species. For example, a species that is sometimes seen in the local fish store at about 4 or 5 inches (10.2 to 12.7 cm) is the "bumblebee grouper." As the name implies, this fish has a strikingly beautiful banded pattern of yellow, black, and white—and you might be tempted to purchase it. However, this cute little fish is really the giant grouper, *Epinephelus lanceolatus*, an Indo-Pacific giant that tops 8 feet (244 cm)! Buyer beware! There are, however, some true groupers that are much smaller and, though almost all of them still need a big tank (125 gallons [472 L] or more), they are not completely beyond the means of the serious home aquarist.

Once we move beyond the groupers, we come to an assortment of smaller species, including many with aquarium potential: the basslets (mostly genera *Gramma* and *Serranus*), dottybacks (mostly genus *Pseudochromis*), and hamlets (genus *Hypoplectrus*). Most of these fish are in the range of 3 to 6 inches (7.6 to 15.2 cm), so aquarium space is not a problem. But, these small fish can sometimes pack a big attitude, particularly some of the dottybacks, so managing aggression can be an issue.

Miniatus Grouper

Although its size is at the upper end of what can be considered "keepable" in the home aquarium, I must admit that the miniatus grouper is one of my favorite marine fish, which I consider a hardy species recommended for large tanks. With its incredible color pattern of electric-blue polka dots against an orange-red body, this is arguably the most gorgeous of the true groupers available to the aquarist.

As with many other groupers, the miniatus grouper has a distinct personality and will endear itself to its keeper. I was watching one, at the local fish store just last night, which came to the front of the tank and eyed me as if to say, "Food?" I moved my index finger back and forth and the grouper followed the motion with its eyes.

 MINIATUS GROUPER

Cephalopholis miniata

Geographic Range:
Western Pacific;
Indian Ocean; Red Sea

Adult Size: 18 inches
(45 cm)

Temperament: very aggressive with conspecifics, peaceful with other fish of similar size or larger

Food: chunky seafoods are favorites, but will eat most anything meaty

The miniatus grouper is just about the fastest fish I've ever seen. I have seen a small specimen dash from the far end of a 55-gallon (208-L) tank, grab a feeder fish, and retreat to its lair in under a second. Indeed, the miniatus grouper is a ravenous feeder that accepts all chunky seafoods after it is acclimated. It may take a few feeder fish to get it started, but after a while the miniatus grouper will eat almost anything. I have even seen them snap at tiny brine shrimp! Like other red fish, you should make sure this fish gets enough carotenoids in its diet to maintain its bright color.

The miniatus grouper is a dedicated fish eater and cannot be trusted with any other fish it can swallow. With fish its own size and larger, however, it is fairly peaceful, except that it will vigorously defend its lair against intruders, regardless of their size. It also will fight with conspecifics, so only one miniatus can be kept per tank.

The miniatus grouper will often do a lot of digging to construct its own lair, and with a large specimen this can be somewhat disruptive; this is perhaps the only real negative with this species. On the other hand, its sturdiness in captivity makes this a highly recommended species for the aquarist with sufficient space to house it.

Flagtail Grouper

This is one of the most common groupers in the aquarium trade, and you will almost always be able to obtain it from your local fish store. This small grouper has an orange-red forebody, shading to maroon near the tail, which is marked with pennantlike white stripes that give this fish its common name—the flagtail grouper. In terms of care, this fish is similar to the miniatus grouper but has the advantage of its smaller adult size, so it can be kept indefinitely in an aquarium as small as 55 gallons (208 L). Flagtails are hardy and disease resistant, eat all foods, and are peaceful with fish of similar size, except for conspecifics. Like all groupers, they appreciate having a lair to which they can retreat when startled, but they are somewhat less shy than most other aquarium-sized groupers and will usually spend a lot of time in the open from the very beginning.

 FLAGTAIL GROUPER

Cephalopholis urodeta

Geographic Range: Western Pacific; Indian Ocean

Adult Size: 12 inches (30 cm)

Temperament: peaceful with fish of similar size but aggressive with conspecifics

Food: all meaty items

Tobacco Bass

The tobacco bass, named for the orange-brown stripe on its flank, is one of the most available and reasonably priced basslets you will see at your local fish store. This species inhabits sandy flats and slopes and tends to be less secretive in the aquarium than some other *Serranus*. In the wild it is mostly a fish eater, but it is not belligerent toward fish it cannot swallow. It can even be kept in conspecific groups (three to six specimens) as long as you make sure that all individuals are closely matched in size and you introduce them all to the

TOBACCO BASS

Serranus tabacarius

Geographic Range: Caribbean

Adult Size: 6 inches (15 cm)

Temperament: can be kept with conspecifics; peaceful with other species

Food: live brine shrimp and glass shrimp, frozen or freeze-dried krill and bloodworms, small pieces of all meaty seafoods

aquarium at the same time. This normally prevents any single fish from getting the upper hand over its companions. Tobacco bass will thrive on all the usual small live and frozen foods, including mysids, krill, brine shrimp, bloodworms, and finely chopped pieces of larger foods such as squid and scallops.

Harlequin Bass

Although it is not the most colorful of the *Serranus* basslets, the harlequin bass has always been my favorite. It has emerald-green eyes, barred sides, and black-spotted fins. Large specimens develop an attractive yellow wash on the throat and belly. They inhabit rocky or rubble-strewn reefs in shallow water, where they are usually the most common basslet.

I think I am attracted to this species because of its unusual behaviors, some of which are quite rare in sea bass, miniature or otherwise. Adult harlequin bass are usually found as mated pairs that cooperatively defend their territory. They even hunt together, with one fish driving prey toward the other, not unlike lions on the savannah. In my opinion, they do have an undeniable catlike aspect, and they definitely give the aquarist the impression of uncommon intelligence.

Harlequin bass can be kept with a wide variety of other small fish, as long as you take care to ensure none are bite-sized. The aquarium should have a complex aquascape with tons of nooks and crannies for these fish to explore. If you have such a setup, you can try to create a mated pair. Like all *Serranus*, harlequin bass are simultaneous hermaphrodites, meaning that they have functional male and female reproductive organs. Therefore, there is no need to try to determine

⭐ HARLEQUIN BASS

Serranus tigrinus

Geographic Range: Western Atlantic; Caribbean

Adult Size: 5 inches (12.5 cm)

Temperament: will sometimes form mated pairs, but unpaired individuals will quarrel with conspecifics; generally peaceful with fishes too large to swallow

Food: live glass shrimp; frozen or freeze-dried krill, brine shrimp, and mysids; finely chopped meaty seafoods

if an individual is male or female. All of them are both. If you introduce two specimens of exactly the same size at the same time, and if there are hiding places to allow them to retreat while they get acquainted, you may be lucky enough to see them forge a stable relationship.

Harlequin bass feed mostly on shrimp and other small crustaceans, and in the aquarium they will feed on brine shrimp, krill, and mysids. For a special treat, get some live glass shrimp and you may be able to watch a harlequin bass stalking its prey in the natural way.

Blue Hamlet

The hamlets of the genus *Hypoplectrus* are something of an enigma. Depending on which ichthyologist's work you read, hamlets may consist of a single, incredibly variable species (usually assigned to *H. unicolor*) or may include up to a dozen or so separate species. Part of the problem is that the varieties (or species) freely interbreed and there are many intermediate forms. The most recent work, which includes genetic and molecular data, indicates that the hamlets may indeed consist of many species. One or another of these species can be found throughout most of the tropical Western Atlantic and Caribbean.

Hamlets often appear to mimic a number of other fish, including some *Chromis* damselfish and angelfish. The species we'll consider here as representative of the group, the blue hamlet (*H. gemma*), is possibly a mimic of the blue chromis (*Chromis cyanea*).

BLUE HAMLET

Hypoplectrus gemma

Geographic Range: Florida to Belize

Adult Size: 5 inches (12.5 cm)

Temperament: aggressive with conspecifics but peaceful with unrelated species

Food: live glass shrimp; frozen or freeze-dried krill, brine shrimp, and mysids; finely chopped meaty seafoods

The blue hamlet is probably the most common species (or variety) seen in the hobby, and they are usually inexpensive. You should be able to obtain one easily from your local fish store. They are aggressive toward similar-looking conspecifics, though sometimes you can get away with keeping more than one species or variety. They require plenty of rockwork to feel secure and may be very shy at first. Frequently, blue hamlets are a bit reluctant to feed at first, but live glass shrimp will usually get them through the first week or so. Gradually introduce some krill or mysids along with the live shrimp and then slowly reduce the number of live shrimp per feeding. Soon, you should be able to wean hamlets off the shrimp and get them eating most meaty fresh and frozen seafoods. Once acclimated, hamlets prove hardy and peaceful and often live for many years.

Six-Lined Grouper

Although called a grouper, *G. sexlineatus* is technically one of the related soapfish, which secrete a toxic body slime to discourage predators. The name describes what may happen if you put a stressed-out specimen into a small container—it will produce so much of the toxic slime that it forms soaplike suds. This toxin is intended to irritate the mouth and gills of a predator, so that it will release a soapfish it has grabbed, and also induces severe breathing difficulties in fish. Unfortunately, if a soapfish freaks out and produces toxic suds in the small, closed system of the aquarium, this defense becomes a true "weapon of mass destruction" that may suffocate every fish in the tank—including the soapfish! (Truth be told, the soapfish rarely uses its weapon of mass destruction, but you must be careful not to stress it into doing so.)

Grammistes sexlineatus

Geographic Range: Western Pacific; Indian Ocean

Adult Size: 12 inches (30 cm)

Temperament: will eat fishes even its own size, including conspecifics; may release toxin when stressed or attacked

Food: will eat anything except vegetable matter; a greedy eater prone to obesity

This fish of rocky reef slopes and flats adapts well to the aquarium. It is a ravenous eater that is prone to becoming obese, so be careful not to overfeed. It will eat just about anything except vegetable matter, and it will probably even sample that before spitting it out. This soapfish has a large mouth and is capable of eating fish nearly its own size, including conspecifics. However, if you can deal with its rapacious appetite and select its tankmates carefully, this is a very durable fish that frequently lives for many years in captivity.

Diadem Dottyback

This small dottyback is a standard item in shipments from Indonesia and the Philippines. It is bright yellow with a pink to purple dorsal stripe, so its beauty, as well as the fact that it is inexpensive, makes it a common purchase for the beginning hobbyist.

Unfortunately, this is a pugnacious species that often creates problems for its keeper. It will often mercilessly harass fish about its own size, especially those of similar color, and conspecifics are a definite no-no (despite the fact that *P. diadema* are often found in conspecific groups in the wild). When the dottyback is kept with much larger and very dissimilar fish, such as many angelfish and butterflyfish, you stand a better chance of managing the aggression of this little tyrant.

The diadem dottyback is very hardy and will take all small foods such as mysids and brine shrimp. This is yet another species that needs careful and constant vitamin and mineral supplementation to maintain its bright colors; many specimens seen in the local fish store have pale, washed-out pastel colors that do not compare with the intensity of newly imported fish.

DIADEM DOTTYBACK

Pictichromis diadema

Geographic Range: Western Pacific

Adult Size: 2.5 inches (6.25 cm)

Temperament: harasses fish of similar size and color, especially conspecifics

Food: all small meaty foods such as mysids

Orchid Dottyback

The electric-purple orchid dottyback is the best dottyback currently available to the aquarist, for a number of reasons. First, the majority of the specimens seen for sale are now captive bred. Second, it is relatively mild mannered; it coexists well with other species, and even gets along with conspecifics with a minimum amount of squabbling if the tank is large and loaded with hiding places. Finally, its colors usually do not fade like those of many other dottybacks, although it should still be given a varied diet of mysids, brine shrimp, bloodworms, krill, and similar items that simulate the planktonic crustaceans it would feed on in the wild.

 ORCHID DOTTYBACK

Pseudochromis fridmani

Geographic Range: Red Sea

Adult Size: 4 inches (10 cm)

Temperament: initially shy and prone to being bullied, mild-mannered with other species with slight aggression toward conspecifics

Food: mysids, brine shrimp, bloodworms, krill, and finely chopped meaty seafoods of all kinds

Orchid dottybacks are fairly shy at first and need many hiding places to feel comfortable. They are prone to being bullied by larger fish and will stop feeding if they are constantly harassed. Ideal tank-mates include small gobies, fairy wrasses, and other nonaggressive species. They should not be kept with fish of similar coloration, such as the magenta dottyback (*Pictichromis porphyraea*) or the blackcap basslet (*Gramma melacara*).

Royal Gramma

The royal gramma is certainly one of the most recognizable marine fish, and is probably the most available basslet in the hobby (though in recent years has been getting some competition from the dotty-backs for the top spot). Its magenta head and yellow tail merge into each other at the midbody with a transitional mix of yellow and magenta scales.

The royal gramma inhabits caves and overhangs, typically on steep reef slopes and cliffs. Sometimes found in large groups, they often orient themselves upside down with their bellies close to the roof of their lair. In the aquarium they require numerous hiding places, and they are often light-shy at first, with this tendency decreasing over time. Royal grammas are hardy, long-lived, and ideal even for the most novice hobbyist.

Royal grammas are good neighbors with most other small fish, yet they will guard their refuge from all intruders by vigorous head shaking and gill flaring. They can be kept in groups as long as you are ready to remove any individual that may be bullied by a more dominant one. Keeping groups may enable you to observe their spawning, which is not uncommon in the aquarium. A male, which has a larger body and head than a female, will construct a nest from

 ROYAL GRAMMA

Gramma loreto

Geographic Range: Caribbean

Adult Size: 3.5 inches (8.75 cm)

Temperament: peaceful with smaller fish, generally quite territorial with conspecifics

Food: mysids, brine shrimp, bloodworms, krill, and finely chopped meaty seafoods

stands of filamentous ("hair") algae and bits of larger macroalgae. He will entice a female to his lair, and she will lay up to 100 or so eggs that the male then guards. Once the eggs hatch, however, no further parental care is given. The planktonic larvae will feed on rotifers (small, multicellular plankton) and soon graduate to brine shrimp nauplii. Although royal grammas are difficult for the home aquarist to raise, commercial hatcheries are now raising good numbers of them, and captive-bred stock is available. Please consider purchasing captive-bred over wild specimens when you have the choice. Captive-bred fish have an edge over wild-caught in terms of hardiness.

Marine Betta

Almost every local fish store sells this species under the name of "marine betta" because of its habit of flaring its fins in a manner not unlike that of the freshwater Siamese fighting fish (*Betta spendens*). I prefer the alternative common name, comet, which I think more accurately describes the fish's color pattern of starry white spots against a dark brown body. Also notable is the large ocellus ("eyespot") at the base of the soft dorsal fin; some researchers believe that this is intended to mimic the appearance of a large, spotted moray eel, thus conferring upon the comet some protection from predators.

Comets are members of the family Plesiopidae, a collection of grouper relatives often known as hardyheads or longfins. In the aquarium, as in the wild, they are nocturnal lurkers. While they will learn to come out for food, they rarely lose their shyness and must be provided with caves and, preferably, a dimly lit tank.

I have kept *C. altivelis* on several occasions and can confirm what many other authors have said about its hardiness. It appears to be nearly bulletproof in its resistance to disease, and will often be

★ MARINE BETTA

Calloplesiops altivelis

Geographic Range:
Western Pacific;
Eastern Indian Ocean

Adult Size: 8 inches
(20 cm)

Temperament:
extremely shy and
peaceful

Food: glass shrimp,
mysids, thawed frozen
krill, small chunks of
all meaty seafoods

unscathed by outbreaks of protozoan or bacterial infections that affect every other inhabitant of a tank.

Calloplesiops often are slow to begin feeding in captivity, and they must be kept with placid tankmates that will not disturb them in their caves or gulp down the lion's share of the food before the slower comet can get to it. It is interesting to watch comets stalk prey such as guppies or glass shrimp. They approach sideways, with fins flared. It has always seemed to me that they were attempting to use the fins and body as a net to corral and trap prey. Although glass shrimp should always be a staple food item, most comets will eventually take to krill, mysids, and similar items.

CARDINALFISH

The cardinalfish (family Apogonidae) have always been among my favorites, partly because I believe the family has many species of underappreciated aquarium potential. There are about 12 genera and more than 200 species in Apogonidae. They inhabit all temperate and subtropical seas, and there are even a few freshwater species. Most cardinals reach an adult length of between 2 and 4 inches (5 to 10.2 cm), and they are superficially like little squirrelfish—big-eyed nocturnal predators that feed on small plankton and the occasional small fish. (By contrast, one genus, *Cheilodipterus*, bucks the family trend by consisting of aggressive fish eaters, some of which reach 10 inches [25 cm] in size.) A number of species seek shelter in spiny and/or venomous invertebrates such as sea urchins.

Cardinalfish are mouthbrooders, with the male taking on the incubation of the eggs. Although many species will readily spawn in captivity, I am aware of only one—the Bangaii cardinalfish (*Pterapogon kauderni*)—that is successfully reared on a regular basis.

Cardinalfish prefer to school under overhangs shielded from direct light. Most species are rather shy and retiring, and they do not do well if their tankmates are active and pugnacious. (That means no damselfish, for the most part.) They are good companions for gobies, smaller basslets, and most pygmy angelfish and smaller butterflyfish. Small shrimp will be devoured, but larger crustaceans and most soft-bodied invertebrates will be left alone.

Cardinalfish are not notably sensitive or especially prone to disease problems. On the odd occasion that they are stricken with an infection or parasitic problem, they usually respond well to standard medications.

Flame Cardinalfish

Even more so than other cardinals, the flame cardinalfish looks superficially like a small squirrelfish because of its bright red color. It can be kept in aquariums as small as 20 to 30 gallons (75.7 to 114 L). *Apogon maculatus* is an exception to the general rule of cardinalfish sociability; it is a solitary species that should be kept in a tank without other cardinalfish, conspecifics, or otherwise. It will coexist peacefully, however, with almost all unrelated species of similar size. This species is inexpensive and readily available in the aquarium trade, with most specimens coming out of Florida.

Perhaps even more so than the squirrelfish, *A. maculatus* is prone to losing its color in the aquarium, and this seems to happen rapidly. Sometimes, specimens that have only been in captivity for a few

⭐ FLAME CARDINALFISH

Apogon maculatus

Geographic Range: Western Atlantic; Caribbean

Adult Size: 4 inches (10 cm)

Temperament: aggressive with conspecifics, peaceful with unrelated species of similar size

Food: glass shrimp, brine shrimp, krill, pellet foods

weeks have already faded to a dull pink, not the vibrant red seen in freshly collected individuals. Brine shrimp, krill, and color-enhancing pelleted foods, all of which they will accept, will restore their color—but it takes longer to restore it than it does to lose it.

Pajama Cardinalfish

The pajama cardinalfish, or "PJ cardinal" for short, looks like a fish whose color was designed by a committee! How else could we have ended up with this seemingly improbable combination of a yellow head, a black belt across the midbody, and maroon polka dots on the rear half of the body?

This cardinalfish is unusual in a number of other ways, too, that make it an even more suitable aquarium fish than some other species. It is not secretive or light-shy, schools more or less peacefully with conspecifics, and is completely peaceful with other fish. Groups can be kept in the aquarium and will school happily in brightly lit, open water, often far from cover. When they do seek shelter, however, it is usually by diving into thickets of branching *Acropora* corals.

The PJ cardinal is one of the toughest marine fish around and has an almost legendary resistance to disease. This fish usually survives even the laziest keeper's abuse (not that this is any excuse for lackluster care!). They will eat pretty much anything and just go on for years in the aquarium. This is not only the best cardinalfish for the beginner, but is also one of the best marine fish for the beginner, period.

 PAJAMA CARDINALFISH

Sphaeramia nematoptera

Geographic Range: Indian Ocean; Western Pacific

Adult Size: 4 inches (10 cm)

Temperament: social

Food: almost all meat-based live, fresh, frozen, or prepared foods

Bangaii Cardinalfish

In 1994, the Bangaii cardinalfish, which was known to science but not known to aquarists, was rediscovered in a remote area of Indonesia. It has been a hot commodity in the aquarium trade ever since, for several reasons. Certainly, one reason is that it is a beautiful fish with a striped black-and-white body accentuated by star-like white spangles and long, elegant fins. Additionally, it has proven to be hardy, feeding eagerly on all standard foods, and to be active by day in much the same manner as *Sphaeramia nematoptera*.

But the main reason for the Bangaii cardinalfish's popularity is an oddity of its reproduction. Like all cardinalfish, *P. kauderni* is a mouthbrooder. But when the eggs have hatched, the male does not simply spit out planktonic larvae to be carried away by the currents; rather, he continues to take the young back into his mouth to protect them for at least the first two weeks. This is completely unique among marine fish. Only *P. kauderni* is known to completely lack a

---

 ## BANGAII CARDINALFISH

Pterapogon kauderni

Geographic Range: Vicinity of Bangaii Island, Sulawesi, Indonesia

Adult Size: 3.5 inches (8.75 cm)

Temperament: peaceful and shy

Food: almost all meat-based live, fresh, frozen, or prepared foods

---

larval stage and provide posthatching parental care. The Bangaii cardinalfish's reproductive behavior resembles that of a mouthbrooding cichlid more than it does any other marine fish. This means that it is probably the easiest marine fish to breed successfully in captivity, because there are no larvae that require odd and hard-to-raise foods such as rotifers. When released from their father's mouth, the babies are about a quarter inch in length and can immediately be fed brine shrimp nauplii.

Bangaii cardinalfish are found in shallow waters, often among seagrass beds. Their color pattern is apparently an adaptation that helps them camouflage themselves in or near long-spined *Diadema* sea urchins, although they also associate with several species of giant anemones, much as clownfish (also called the anemonefish) do. In fact, sometimes they will actually share a large anemone with the clownfish, apparently without conflict.

Because they do not have larvae that drift away with the current to colonize new areas, the Bangaii cardinalfish is restricted to a small

○ Though most butterflyfish typically are aggressive toward conspecifics, these golden butterflies stay together as a mated pair.

geographic area and is uniquely vulnerable to overcollecting. There was (and is) concern that collecting would have a negative impact on the population, but so far the available evidence indicates that this is not the case. However, you can help make sure this never happens by insisting that specimens you buy are captive bred. Because it is perhaps the only marine fish that even the most casual breeder can successfully raise, it would be extremely irresponsible to decimate the wild population.

BUTTERFLYFISH

Butterflyfish are some of the most conspicuous and spectacular fish on the coral reef. The 130 or so species are mostly tropical, although a few species come from cooler temperate waters. These flattened, disc-shaped, or triangular fish are indeed well-named, because they resemble butterflies at rest with folded wings. By and large, they are brightly colored and cruise serenely over a reef as butterflies do over a meadow.

The family name, Chaetodontidae, means "comb-toothed," referring to the tiny, brushlike teeth that are used to pick and graze a variety of small food items, depending on species. Those teeth, and the dietary habits that come with them, are the bane of many an aquarist's existence; for the butterflyfish include the full range of aquarium adaptability, from species that are nearly bulletproof to species that are absolutely, positively, 100 percent "unkeepable"—and everything in-between those two extremes. Some butterflyfish feed only on living coral polyps, and these species are completely unkeepable. Still other species feed on a wider variety of invertebrates and algae, and, thus, are very suited to aquarium life. Even so, butterflyfish can be finicky feeders. Even for species that will adapt to an aquarium diet, it may take some patience and experimentation with a wide variety of foods to get them started feeding.

A few species of butterflyfish form schools, but most are found on the reef as mated pairs. Unless you can obtain a mated pair (which will cost you a pretty penny—up to hundreds of dollars depending on the species), most butterflyfish are aggressive toward conspecifics and sometimes even toward other butterflyfish species. In general, then, it is best to keep just one to a tank. Butterflyfish are rarely belligerent toward unrelated species, however, and are good community fish. In fact, it requires care and careful selection to ensure that their tankmates do not bully them. Although butterflyfish are large, they are shy and will not compete well with pugnacious species. Even a small damselfish may harass a large butterfly to death.

Unlike many of the species we've covered so far, the majority of butterflyfish are not light-shy and are active by day in mostly shallow, sunlit waters. (There are also a number of rare and expensive deep-water species.) "Butterflies" are active swimmers and require a lot of open room. Although they need some coral or rocky cover for security and to graze from (they often pick at many decor items in a constant search for food), the decor can be sparser than for the various crevice and cave dwellers we've discussed.

One downside of butterflyfish is that they are more prone to diseases and parasite problems than some of the other fish we've studied. They are often infested with gill flukes, which they attempt to dislodge by scratching. Avoid purchasing any butterfly that scratches! They are also susceptible to ich, though this usually can be cleared up with copper. Because of their increased potential for health problems, butterflyfish must be quarantined after you purchase them—no exceptions! (See Chapter 5 for details on "scratching" and quarantining your fish.)

Raccoon Butterflyfish

Many butterflyfish have a black band obscuring the eye, but in *C. lunula* the band forms a raccoonlike mask. In the wild this is a social butterflyfish that often forms nocturnally foraging shoals, but this behavior rarely carries over to the aquarium, where conspecifics will usually fight. Only in large public aquariums, where large groups can be maintained, will you see something approaching the natural social behavior. Raccoon butterflyfish are almost completely peaceful with non-butterfly species.

This is one of the two or three hardiest butterflies for the marine aquarium. Part of the reason for this is that *C. lunula* is an omnivorous, opportunistic feeder that will eat pieces or whole invertebrates including anemones, hard and soft corals, worms, the tube feet of echinoderms, and a variety of crustaceans. They will also graze on algae, consume fish eggs, and pretty much sample whatever they can.

This is a large species and requires a correspondingly large tank; smaller specimens (3 to 4 inches [7.6 to 10.2 cm]) will adapt to a 55-gallon (208 L) tank, but as they grow they will need to move to tanks in the range of 75 to 100 gallons (284 to 379 L) or more.

 RACCOON BUTTERFLYFISH

Chaetodon lunula

Geographic Range: Indo-Pacific

Adult Size: 8 inches (20 cm)

Temperament: aggressive with conspecifics and sometimes with other butterfly species; peaceful with non-butterfly species

Food: mysids, krill, brine shrimp, bloodworms, and finely diced meaty seafoods; may also pick at filamentous algae and macroalgae

Sunburst Butterflyfish

This is the single best butterflyfish for the marine aquarium. Like the raccoon butterflyfish, it consumes a varied diet of invertebrates and algae and will accept virtually all aquarium foods. It has greater resistance to disease than any other butterflyfish, and for this reason alone I recommend it as your first butterflyfish.

Additionally, the sunburst butterflyfish is less aggressive toward conspecifics than almost any other butterfly. It takes a large tank, 75 gallons (284 L) and up, to keep a group, but it is worth the effort. Your odds for success will be better if you purchase six or more butterflies, rather than two or three; if all the individuals in the group

SUNBURST BUTTERFLYFISH

Chaetodon kleinii

Geographic Range:
Indo-Pacific

Adult Size: 6 inches
(15 cm)

Temperament: can be kept with con-specifics; peaceful toward other species

Food: mysids, krill, brine shrimp, blood-worms, and finely diced meaty seafoods; may even eat flake foods and small pellet foods

are closely matched in size; and if they are all introduced to the aquarium at the same time—as you should do with other semisocial species.

Yellow Longnose Butterflyfish

This delicate-looking animal is actually one of the hardiest species of butterflyfish. I would place it as a close second to the sunburst but-

 YELLOW LONGNOSE BUTTERFLYFISH

Forcipiger flavissimus

Geographic Range:
Indo-Pacific

Adult Size: 8 inches
(20 cm)

Temperament: cannot be kept with con-specifics and may be aggressive with other butterfly species; peaceful with all oth-ers unless attacked

Food: mysids, brine shrimp, bloodworms; extremely small pieces of all meaty seafoods

terflyfish in terms of overall adaptability and hardiness. With its long, slender snout, it looks like an exclusive eater of coral polyps, but in reality the snout is used like a pair of forceps to snip the legs and antennae off of shrimp and small crabs, to pluck the exposed tentacles from tubeworms, to clip tentacle tips from anemones and corals, and to probe into almost any crevice for hidden microcrustaceans and other tiny foods.

Unless you can obtain a mated pair, this is another species that should not be kept with conspecifics, and it sometimes behaves aggressively toward other butterflyfish, too. It is peaceful with all other fish but will defend itself by raising its stout dorsal spines if attacked.

Bannerfish

The bannerfish is an unusual butterflyfish that feeds mostly on zooplankton in the water column. With its bold, black-and-white stripes and tall dorsal fin, the bannerfish resembles the Moorish idol (*Zanclus canescens*), a prized but delicate fish that should definitely be avoided by the beginner. Thankfully, the bannerfish is very tough. It is pretty disease resistant for a butterflyfish, eats just about anything, and is more forgiving of moderate water quality variations than most of its kin.

Bannerfish are often available at your local fish store at a size of only 2 to 3 inches (5 to 7.6 cm), but this is a potentially large fish and should eventually be kept in tanks of 125 gallons (473 L) and larger. Bannerfish do well in groups, with the usual precautions: make sure they are all about the same size, and preferably introduce them all to the tank at the same time.

 BANNERFISH

Heniochus acuminatus

Geographic Range: Indo-Pacific

Adult Size: 10 inches (25 cm)

Temperament: social

Food: mysids, brine shrimp, bloodworms, finely chopped scallop and squid

ANGELFISH

There are about seventy-five species of marine angelfish (family Pomacanthidae), found primarily in tropical and subtropical seas worldwide. They are similar in many respects to the butterflyfish and were once grouped with them in a single large family; however, there are some important differences. Perhaps the most visible difference is the large spine on the preopercle (forward gill cover) that angels possess and butterflies lack.

Like butterflyfish, many angelfish are brightly colored, tend to be found as mated pairs or harems (a male with a group of females) in the wild, and are small-mouthed grazers. They feed on encrusting (coralline) and filamentous algae, hydroids, and other fixed (sessile) invertebrates—and a number of species feed largely on sponges. Also like butterflyfish, they are extremely variable in their captive hardiness. Some species are among the easiest of marine fish to keep, while others refuse all foods and will slowly waste away in captivity.

The most common genera in the aquarium trade are the large *Pomacanthus* and *Holacanthus*, and the pygmy angels, *Centropyge*. The pygmies are the most ideal for the aquarium, so we'll look at them first.

⊕ Note the horizontal striping on this near-adult emperor angelfish. Juveniles of this species display more of a circular pattern (still faintly visible on this specimen) and are mostly blue and white.

Cherubfish

The cherubfish is the smallest of the pygmy angels, which makes it the smallest marine angelfish overall. An attractive little fish, it is basically a solid deep blue with a yellow head. In contrast to its

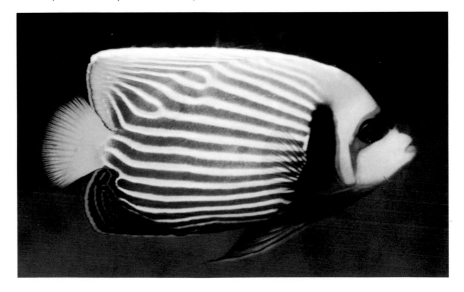

name, however, this is a little devil of a fish. Because of its size, it can be kept in tanks as small as 15 or 20 gallons (57 to 76 L), but if you do it must be the only fish, because it will harass any tankmate. Unlike some other species, it will not limit its aggression to conspecifics, but will attack pretty much any other fish. Therefore, despite its diminutive size, a tank of 55 gallons (208 L) and larger is recommended to successfully integrate the cherubfish into a community. Even then, the cherubfish should be added last so that the other residents have the advantage of staking out their territories first. They'll need that advantage!

CHERUBFISH

Centropyge argi

Geographic Range: Western Atlantic; Caribbean

Adult Size: 3 inches (7.5 cm)

Temperament: Very aggressive; should only be kept with larger species in a large tank; may be lethally aggressive toward conspecifics and other pygmy angels

Food: nori and all other vegetable-based foods; will also eat brine shrimp, mysids, bloodworms

Aside from its feisty nature, there is much to recommend about *C. argi* as an aquarium fish. As we have noted, it is small, but it is also reasonably priced—probably the cheapest *Centropyge* you will see—and commonly available. It is also long-lived (usually more than five years, sometimes much more) in captivity and resistant to most diseases. As with all angels, though, be on the lookout for gill flukes in freshly imported specimens.

Cherubfish are almost exclusively herbivorous; they will eat filamentous algae, diatoms, and even blue-green bacteria ("slime algae"). Feed them a variety of green foods and make sure there is always some nori clipped inside the tank.

Coral Beauty

The coral beauty is the ideal first angelfish for the marine aquarist. Although not 100 percent placid, it is probably the most peaceful

Centropyge and will get along well with most tankmates, as long as there are no conspecifics. It is also the hardiest of its clan and is not overly prone to disease. It is common in the trade and perhaps only a few dollars more expensive than a cherubfish.

The coral beauty is incredibly variable. Most have a purple head and purple fins (except for orange or yellow pelvic fins), with some rusty color and thin darker bars on the flanks. However, depending on the geographic location where they are collected, some individuals will be almost all purple and some mostly rusty in color.

In the aquarium, the coral beauty, like all *Centropyge*, does best if provided with large amounts of aquascaping. These fish are adept at navigating through small crevices, disappearing at one end of the tank, and popping up at the opposite end. They are also challenging for collectors to capture on the reef.

Offer a variety of vegetable-based foods and some occasional feeding of brine shrimp to keep a coral beauty happy and healthy.

 CORAL BEAUTY

Centropyqe bispinosus

Geographic Range: Indo-Pacific

Adult Size: 4 inches (10 cm)

Temperament: cannot be kept with conspecifics; generally peaceful with other species

Food: anything vegetable-based, brine shrimp

Flame Angelfish

The truly amazing color of the flame angelfish has made it a must-have for every local fish store, and almost every marine hobbyist will keep this species sooner or later. With its luminous red-orange body, black stripes, and blue-tipped dorsal and anal fins, it's easy to see why this fish is so popular. It is more expensive than the previous two species, but still well within the range of most hobbyists. Specimens from Hawaii tend to be the most intensely colored and command higher prices. In some pygmy angelfish, it is possible to distinguish the sexes. In the flame angelfish, males have more blue on the dorsal and anal fin tips. Like most *Centropyge*, *C. loriculus* tends to be

⭐ FLAME ANGELFISH

Centropyge loriculus

Geographic Range:
Central and Western
Pacific

Adult Size: 4 inches
(10 cm)

Temperament:
Moderately aggressive
with other species;
very aggressive with
conspecifics in a small
tank but can be kept
in a harem arrange-
ment in large tanks

Food: greens, brine
shrimp, mysids

intolerant of conspecifics; but if you have the money to experiment, you could try to duplicate the harem social structure that this species exhibits in the wild: In a large tank (125 gallons [473 L] or larger), introduce one male and three to four females at the same time. A male guards a large territory that encompasses the smaller territories of his harem of females. There must be many, many hiding places for this to have a chance of working, and you should be ready to remove a badly harassed individual at any time. If it works, though, you will have an unusual and beautiful display.

Flame angels are moderately aggressive, falling somewhere between the extremes represented by *C. argi* and *C. bispinosus*. In most aquariums that are large enough (30 gallons [114 L] and up) and not heavily stocked, aggression will be manageable.

The flame angel is another algae browser, so offer nori constantly and feed a wide variety of other greens.

King Angelfish

The large angelfish of the genus *Holacanthus* are somewhat rectangular in shape, with magnificent long filaments trailing from the dorsal and anal fins of mature specimens. *Holacanthus* angels are among the most colorful and conspicuous inhabitants of rocky and coral reefs of the Western Atlantic and Eastern Pacific. A number of species are seen in the hobby, but the king angelfish is arguably the most hardy and will serve here as the best representative of the genus.

The king angelfish is indeed beautiful, with a blue body, white midbody stripe, and bright yellow tail. The sexes are distinguishable: the pelvic fins are white in the male, and yellow in the female. This species is extraordinarily hardy, but is also extremely aggressive, so it needs a large tank (125 gallons [473 L] and up) and tough neighbors. It will generally get along reasonably well with triggerfish, larger groupers, larger morays (*Gymnothorax*), and other rough customers. However, when mixing large, aggressive fish, any cease-fire is subject to change at a moment's notice.

As with all nearly all species of *Holacanthus*, sponges form the bulk of the diet, along with a wide variety of benthic invertebrates and algae. Unlike some other *Holacanthus* species—such as the rock beauty (*H. tricolor*) and the queen angelfish (*H. ciliaris*)—which are fairly delicate and decline without sponges in their diet, *H. passer* thrives on just about any food. However, the inclusion of sponge-based prepared foods is still recommended.

 KING ANGELFISH

Holacanthus passer

Geographic Range: Eastern Pacific, especially Gulf of California

Adult Size: 14 inches (35 cm)

Temperament: very aggressive and hardy; a good tankmate for rough-and-tumble species such as triggerfish

Food: sponge-based frozen diets should be a staple, but will eat anything

Blue Moon Angelfish

I am including this species here because it may be the hardiest of all the marine angelfish, although it is a very large fish that will eventually demand the largest standard-sized aquarium (220 gallons [833 L]). It is also quite expensive. However, it eats anything, and I mean anything, including flakes and pellets, and seems less prone to HLLE and dietary deficiencies than other angels. It is also resistant to most bacterial infections and parasitic problems.

On top of that, it is among the most gorgeous display fish you could hope to keep, with a blue body and namesake half-moons on the head, along with a huge lemon-yellow midbody bar; the adults develop dorsal and anal streamers that may be half the length of the body. They are not the least bit shy, and like to regally cruise the open waters of the aquarium.

Pomacanthus maculosus

Geographic Range: Red Sea, Western Indian Ocean

Adult Size: 20 inches (50 cm)

Temperament: aggressive toward other angelfish species and conspecifics; peaceful with unrelated species

Food: will eat anything, including all prepared foods

Although it may be aggressive toward other angels and must not be kept with conspecifics, *P. maculosus* is usually nonaggressive toward other fish but will compete for the lion's share at feeding time.

If you have the money to obtain and the space to house this fish, there is not a better angelfish you will find.

Koran Angelfish

The Koran angel is probably the most common large angelfish in your local fish store, and perhaps the most reasonably priced, too. Juveniles of 4 to 5 inches (10.2 to 12.7 cm) are usually available and

KORAN ANGELFISH

Pomacanthus semicirculatus

Geographic Range: Western Pacific; Indian Ocean

Adult Size: 14 inches (35 cm)

Temperament: aggressive toward other angelfish species and conspecifics; usually peaceful with unrelated species

Food: sponge-based frozen diets should be a staple, but will eat anything

adapt well to aquarium life. Their bright blue and white stripes will fade to more somber coloration as they reach adulthood, unlike many other *Pomacanthus*, which get more brilliant with age. However, even the adults are attractive fish.

Koran angels can be fairly aggressive; they should be the last fish added to an aquarium to give previous inhabitants a territorial advantage. Tankmates should be of similar size and should not include other angels—Korans or otherwise.

Korans will eat all aquarium foods, including flakes and pellets, with gusto. They should still be offered a wide variety, including large amounts of vegetable matter and occasional feedings of sponge-based preparations, but they are not fussy.

DAMSELFISH

Damselfish (family Pomacentridae) are widespread in all tropical seas (some two dozen genera and more than 300 species) but reach their greatest diversity in the Indo-Pacific. One of their unusual features is that they have one nostril on each side of the head, whereas most marine fish have two, for a total of four; they share this feature with the freshwater cichlids, to which they may be distantly related. They certainly have a cichlid-like attitude, too! Though they are small (just 3 to 4 inches [7.2 to 10.2 cm], in many species), damsels are highly territorial and will attack intruders many times their size. Most species are primarily herbivorous; some, particularly *Stegastes* species, actually "farm" patches of filamentous algae for their own consumption. Damsels are opportunistic, however, and, despite their dietary preferences, they'll eat just about anything small.

I would be remiss if I did not mention a special subgroup of damselfish: the clownfish. More correctly known as "anemonefish," they are assigned to their own subfamily, Amphiprioninae. As the name implies, they live in symbiotic association with a number of species of giant sea anemones. Some clownfish species associate with just one species of giant anemone, others with several. There is some ongoing debate about the precise nature of this symbiosis. The term *symbiosis* means "living together," but it comes in many flavors: mutualism, in which both partners benefit from the relationship; commensalism, in which one partner benefits and the other is neither benefited nor harmed; and parasitism, in which one partner benefits and the other is harmed. Obviously, the clownfish benefits by having a safe refuge in the anemone's stinging tentacles. But, does the anemone get anything in return? Clownfish have been observed taking food and placing it in their anemone's tentacles. Are they truly feeding the anemone (meaning a mutualistic relationship), or are they just stashing food inside their lair, as many damsels do, and only accidentally feeding the anemone? The debate continues.

Clownfish also have a fascinating social structure. Clownfish are protandrous ("male first") hermaphrodites. A group of juvenile clownfish will be all males. As they mature, the largest and most dominant fish changes sex to become a functioning female. The next fish down in the hierarchy will become a functioning male and her mate. If the female dies or is removed, the dominant male changes sex and becomes the new "queen" of the group. The next-smallest male then moves up to become the new female's mate. A large anemone may contain many clownfish, usually of a single species, but there will be only one breeding pair; all the others are inactive males.

In the aquarium, most damsels are extremely durable; in fact, they were once commonly used (and sometimes still are) to cycle new tanks. However, when they are used in this way, the damsels have the last laugh. Being the first ones in the tank lets them get the territorial upper hand, and many a cheap damsel has beaten up an expensive display fish many times its size.

To be sure, damsels are attractive and interesting fish in their own right, and there is nothing wrong with keeping them with other damsels if you have a tremendous amount of aquascaping so that harassed individuals can get out of a dominant fish's line of sight. (If you have freshwater experience, you'll know what I mean by this single recommendation: treat them like cichlids.) Where most aquarists run into trouble is in trying to integrate damsels into a community setting with other species. In many cases, the damsels just won't have it.

That being said, let's look at a small assortment of damsels commonly available in your local fish store, starting with several clownfish.

⊛ TOMATO CLOWNFISH

Amphiprion frenatus

Geographic Range: Western Pacific

Adult Size: 6 inches (15 cm)

Temperament: territorial toward intruders but peaceful with tankmates that do not invade its "personal space"; can be kept with conspecifics but will establish a pecking order

Food: mysids, krill, brine shrimp, blood-worms, finely chopped seafoods, most pellet and flake foods

Tomato Clownfish

Juveniles of this species are generally tomato-red (hence the common name), with a single white bar on the head. As they mature, the body darkens to deep maroon or black, but the fins and head stay red. This is an inexpensive and hardy clownfish. In the wild it associates only with the bulb-tipped anemone, *Entacmaea quadricolor*. It does fine, however, in captivity without an anemone.

Although the tomato, like all clowns, will eat flake foods and other dried foods, it will do much better with a variety of zooplankton: mysids, brine shrimp, krill, and the like. Like other red fish, it will maintain brighter colors if it gets plenty of carotenoids from the krill and brine shrimp, although it is not quite as prone to fading as, say, squirrelfish or cardinalfish.

False Percula Clownfish

This is the clownfish starring in the hit Disney/Pixar movie, *Finding Nemo*. Also called an anemonefish, this species is bright orange with three white bars and is similar to only one other fish: the true percula clownfish, *A. percula*. Both are available, but the majority you will see in your local fish store are *A. ocellaris*. To tell them apart, look at the black edging of the white bars, which is hair-thin in *A. ocellaris*, but much thicker in *A. percula*.

In the wild, *A. ocellaris* is found with the anemones *Heteractis magnifica*, *Stichodactyla gigantea*, and *S. mertensii*. All of these

Amphiprion ocellaris

Geographic Range:
Western Pacific;
Eastern Indian Ocean

Adult Size: 4 inches
(10 cm)

Temperament: somewhat territorial toward intruders but shyer than other clownfish species; may not compete effectively with aggressive tankmates; can be kept with conspecifics but will establish a pecking order

Food: mysids, krill, brine shrimp, bloodworms, finely chopped seafoods, most pellet and flake foods

anemones are notoriously difficult to keep in the aquarium, and, unless you have the resources to provide the intense light they require, I recommend that you keep your anemonefish without anemones. There are now highly realistic anemone replicas for sale, and I am curious about whether clownfish will accept these in lieu of the real thing. I can find no data one way or the other, but you could try one of these simulations and see if it works.

Despite what some literature has claimed over the years, my experience is that wild-caught *A. ocellaris* and *A. percula* tend to be delicate, acclimating only slowly, being somewhat disease prone, and not holding their own especially well with tankmates. Captive-bred specimens, however, are now widely available and you should always select these, even if you have to pay a bit more. Captive-bred clowns are tough, hardy, and accept all foods immediately. Although I place it as number three in preference of the clownfish we're covering here, they are still worthy of considering for your tank if you buy only captive-bred.

Maroon Clownfish

The maroon clownfish is sometimes called the spine-cheeked clownfish because it is the only clownfish with a pair of opercular spines; thus, it is placed in a separate genus, *Premnas*. This is a sturdy clownfish with a dark red body and thin white or yellow bars. It does not

★ MAROON CLOWNFISH

Premnas biaculeatus

Geographic Range: Western Pacific; Eastern Indian Ocean

Adult Size: 7 inches (17.5 cm)

Temperament: moderately aggressive and a good tankmate with non-clownfish species

Food: mysids, krill, brine shrimp, bloodworms, finely chopped seafoods, most pellets and flake foods

seem shy without an anemone (in nature it is found only with *E. quadricolor*). Maroon clowns often swim in the open, far from cover. It is somewhat more aggressive than other clowns, but still far less so than the majority of damselfish, so it can hold its own with similar-sized tankmates without being bullied or being a bully.

In my opinion, this species is also the most disease resistant of the clowns. I highly recommend that you start with this species before moving on to other clownfish.

White-Tailed Damselfish

Confusingly, there are two similar black-and-white striped damselfish seen in the trade: *D. aruanus* and *D. melanurus*. For some reason, these are almost always sold as the "three-striped" and "four-striped" damsels, respectively. I recommend that you just look at the tails rather than try to count stripes, and that you use the alternate common names of white-tailed damselfish for *D. aruanus* and black-tailed damselfish for *D. melanurus*. The two species are often mixed together at your local fish store.

Both species hover in large groups above heads of *Acropora* corals, and you can keep groups in a large tank; but be prepared to remove some, as a few will probably come out on the short end of the social hierarchy.

These are disease-resistant damsels that eat all foods and tolerate just about any water conditions. They can be pretty aggressive but are far less so than several other species. In fact, their tenacity can be an advantage. Some aquarists keep them with much larger fish as "dither fish." Dithers are small, fast fish that are deliberately put in

Dascyllus aruanus

Geographic Range: Western Pacific; Indian Ocean

Adult Size: 4 inches (10 cm)

Temperament: moderately aggressive

Food: all foods of appropriate size for their small mouths

harm's way, but usually without any harm coming to them. The purpose of dithers is to divert the aggression of larger fish such as triggerfish and large angels. When the larger fish chase the damsels, the damsels can retreat to the deep recesses of a coral head, while having taken the bully's attention away from other tankmates.

Domino Damselfish

The domino damselfish has a self-explanatory name. It has a velvet-black body (large adults may fade to gray) with a small white spot on each flank and one on the forehead. It is one of only two or three non-clownfish damsels that regularly inhabit anemones (though adults usually abandon this habit).

Dominos are very cheap, almost indestructible, and will eat just about anything. They are also startlingly aggressive. This may be the single most aggressive damselfish species, and also grows to the size of a small dinner plate. Do you see where I'm going with this? Unless you want to keep a single specimen or a mated pair alone, I do not

Dascyllus trimaculatus

Geographic Range: Indo-Pacific

Adult Size: 8 inches (20 cm)

Temperament: Extremely aggressive; not recommended for most tanks or tankmates

Food: all foods of appropriate size for their small mouths

recommend this fish. Its understated beauty and inexpensive price tag have lured many an unsuspecting aquarist to ruin!

Blue-Green Chromis

After the previous species, I hope I haven't sworn you off damsels completely! That would be unfortunate, because now we come to a relatively nonaggressive species, the blue-green chromis (*Chromis viridis*). In fact, virtually all *Chromis* species are schooling fish that hover near coral heads on reef slopes and pluck zooplankton from the water column. The key to their peaceful natures is probably the fact that they are almost nonterritorial except when guarding a nesting site. The blue-green is probably the most easily obtained species of the genus; but at least several more, such as the blue chromis (*C. cyanea*, a Western Atlantic species) and the black-axil chromis *(C. atripectoralis*, from the Indo-Pacific), are also common.

 BLUE-GREEN CHROMIS

Chromis viridis

Geographic Range:
Indo-Pacific

Adult Size: 4 inches (10 cm)

Temperament: nonterritorial (except when breeding); among the most peaceful damsels

Food: all foods of appropriate size for their small mouths, but more plankton than other damsels

Although they will survive when kept singly, all *Chromis* species look best and seem most at ease when kept in groups of at least six. They will establish a pecking order, but it is comparatively rare that any individual will be bullied to death. Even better, *Chromis* are inoffensive with other species and can be trusted in mixed communities.

Offer a variety of small foods: brine shrimp, mysids, bloodworms, glassworms, and finely chopped pieces of just about anything else. Although they are plankton eaters, they will also consume vegetable matter, so you can offer them supplements of green foods as well.

Blue Devil

Now we move back to a more aggressive species. Although it is not nearly as vicious as the domino, the blue devil is well-named. It will stake out a territory over a coral head and defend it against all com-

Chrysiptera cyanea

Geographic Range: Western Pacific; Eastern Indian Ocean

Adult Size: 2.5 inches (6.25 cm)

Temperament: very territorial toward all intruders, especially conspecifics

Food: all foods of appropriate size for their small mouths

ers. It is intolerant of conspecifics, although you may get away with keeping multiple specimens if you have a complex aquascape with many hiding places for the beleaguered. Blue devils can cohabit with larger fish in a large tank; they will chase anything that comes too close, but they are seldom as relentless as dominos.

At least the fish compensates for its belligerence with its electric-blue colors, and some specimens have yellow or orange tails. I'd like to add a plug for a closely related species, the Fiji devil (*C. taupou*), which also has a blue body but with a yellow belly, tail, and dorsal fin. It is a lovely fish, uncommon in the trade but worth obtaining because it is relatively peaceful.

Yellow-Tailed Blue Damselfish

The yellow-tailed blue damselfish (quite a mouthful!) is like a short-bodied version of the blue devil and has bright yellow on the tail and

 YELLOW-TAILED BLUE DAMSELFISH

Chrysiptera parasema

Geographic Range: Indo-Pacific

Adult Size: 2 inches (5 cm)

Temperament: only moderately aggressive toward other species; variably aggressive toward conspecifics

Food: all foods of appropriate size for their small mouths

caudal peduncle. Unlike its relative, it is not very devilish and does well in most community aquariums. It seems variable in its attitude toward conspecifics. Sometimes they fight fiercely, but I have also seen tanks with stable groups.

You'll often see these at your local fish store in mixed groups of "assorted damsels." As evidence of their basically more gentle nature, you'll usually see them getting beaten up by the dominos and other *Dascyllus* damsels, and maybe by their blue devil cousins, too. However, if you can obtain them from tanks where they are not harassed and damaged, these damsels will acclimate quickly to your tank and adapt to all of the usual foods.

HAWKFISH

There are about thirty-five species of hawkfish (family Cirrhitidae), most of which hail from the Indo-Pacific. These unusual fish are "benthic," lacking a functioning swim bladder. A characteristic of the family is that the spines of the first dorsal fin have their tips subdivided into hairline "cirri," hence the family name. The pectoral fins are stout and often have fingerlike projections that help these fish hang on to their perches—and perch they do! Most hawkfish prefer a vantage point atop a coral head or other elevated spot on the reef. When they spy a crustacean or small fish, they swoop down like hawks on their prey.

Hawkfish cannot be trusted with small fish, nor with just about all crustaceans. However, they are hardy, and a number of the smaller species adapt well to the aquarium. Let's examine just a couple of the most unique.

❸ This redspotted hawkfish enjoys resting on the substrate. Hawkfish are happy to make a meal out of shrimp and crab nearby, so don't keep these species if your tank includes crustacean inhabitants.

Flame Hawkfish

This is one of the reddest fish available to the marine aquarist. Although it exists in a large geographic range, it is a staple in Hawaiian shipments. Newly imported specimens are bright scarlet with black stripes at the base of the dorsal fins and black "spectacles" around the eyes. Sadly, like so many of the red fish we've talked about, the flame hawk's colors will fade unless you conscientiously supplement its diet with krill and other carotenoid-rich foods.

★ FLAME HAWKFISH

Neocirrhitus armatus

Geographic Range: Western Pacific

Adult Size: 4 inches (10 cm)

Temperament: will eat all smaller fishes and will eat or dismember ornamental crustaceans and mollusks; territorial toward other bottom-dwelling fish

Food: crustaceans of all kinds, meaty seafoods

The flame hawkfish is a terror to hard-shelled invertebrates. It will eat any shrimp or crab small enough to catch and dismember, will yank hermit crabs from their shells, even manage to extract snails from their shells or just crunch smaller ones. Flame hawks may also attack gobies and other bottom-dwelling fish, so select their tankmates carefully. They can sometimes be kept with conspecifics if cautiously introduced and if there is a size difference. Flame hawks are protogynous ("female first") hermaphrodites, and the larger of a pair of fish introduced to a tank at the same time may develop into a male, while the smaller one remains a female.

Despite their behavioral drawbacks, flame hawks adapt well to aquarium life, and their beauty will keep them popular with hobbyists.

Longnose Hawkfish

The longnose hawkfish looks delicate but is an adaptable fish that does well in the aquarium. Its chain-link pattern of red and white serves to camouflage it well on its preferred perches—red-colored sea fans. It feeds mostly on crustaceans and is adept at working them

LONGNOSE HAWKFISH

Oxycirrhites typus

Geographic Range: Indo-Pacific (including Eastern Pacific)

Adult Size: 5 inches (12.5 cm)

Temperament: will eat small fishes but peaceful with those its own size or larger

Food: mysids, krill, brine shrimp, blood-worms, fine chunks of meaty seafoods

out of small holes, but the longnose also will not hesitate to take small fish and should not be kept with species such as small, cylindrical gobies.

The social structure of the longnose hawkfish is similar to that of the flame hawkfish, meaning that you can try to create stable pairs and even harems through careful introduction. For these fish to display themselves well in the aquarium, make sure you obtain several artificial red sea fans.

WRASSES

The wrasses (family Labridae) are found in all temperate, subtropical, and tropical seas. With an astounding 500+ species in more than 60 genera, it is difficult to generalize about wrasses. They come in just about every possible shape, size, and color. However, all have a protrusible mouth that can be extended outward, along with some of the teeth. Many species have conspicuous canine teeth, many species burrow in sand, and most species are carnivorous, feeding on a wide variety of invertebrates and small fish.

Wrasses, like so many other marine fish, have a reproductive and social order based on sex change. Juveniles, or initial phase fish, can become either functioning males or females, based on social pressures. The most brightly colored individuals are the terminal phase males, sometimes called "supermales," which dominate a harem of females.

Wrasses vary widely in their suitability for the aquarium. There are many attractive species in the family Labridae that remain a manageable size and have peaceful temperaments. However, there are also species that are too large (up to nearly 7 feet [213.2 cm]!) or too aggressive for the home aquarium. Once again, we will look at several ideal species you might see in your local fish store.

❶ While also referred to as the black spot hogfish, there's no mistaking why this red-and-white striped species gets the nickname candystripe hogfish.

Cuban Hogfish

With its hues of red, white, and yellow, the Cuban hogfish is one of the flashiest fish from the Caribbean. It is not inexpensive but is only about half the size of the related Spanish hogfish (*B. rufus*) that hails from the same waters, so it is a more manageable aquarium fish.

Cuban hogfish are bold fish that display well in an aquarium. They do not need numerous hiding places, just plenty of room to swim. Like most wrasses, they have an odd swimming motion in which only the pectoral fins are used for propulsion; the other fins, including the large tail, are used mostly for steering, if used at all.

The Cuban hog is a good-natured fish that will not attack any but the smallest of tankmates. (As I've said before, any fish will probably attack a tankmate that's bite-sized.) It also lives up to its name—it is a gluttonous eater that will always be the first to arrive at feeding time.

 CUBAN HOGFISH

Bodianus pulchellus

Geographic Range: Western Atlantic; Caribbean

Adult Size: 10 inches (25 cm)

Temperament: peaceful with similar sized tankmates, but its outgoing behavior at feeding time may be intimidating for some tankmates

Food: anything meaty

It likes chunky, meaty foods such as squid, scallops, and large krill, but will also vacuum up even small foods such as brine shrimp. Because of this, it probably should not be kept with butterflies and other picking grazers, which are slow eaters. The faster, gluttonous hogfish (and other species with similar eating habits) will disturb deliberate feeders to the point that they'll stop eating. However, the Cuban hog is a good tank-mate with other wrasses (except conspecifics), large angels, tangs, and other vigorous eaters.

Harlequin Tuskfish

The harlequin tusk is arguably the most striking of the wrasses. A deep-bodied species, it is very different in shape from the more typical torpe-do-shaped wrasses. It is boldly striped with red and white, with green blue from the dorsal fin to the tail, with some blue highlighting on the head and fins—a fish you've got to see to believe. The premium specimens—in terms of appearance, hardiness, and price—come from Australia.

 HARLEQUIN TUSKFISH

Choerodon fasciata

Geographic Range: Indo-Pacific

Adult Size: 8 inches (20 cm)

Temperament: peaceful

Food: glass shrimp, krill, and medium-sized chunks of anything meaty

As the name implies, this wrasse has fearsome tusklike teeth that protrude from the mouth. The thing I think is really weird about this fish is that the teeth have blue stripes! Despite its forbidding appearance, though, this is really a remarkably peaceful fish. I have seen harlequin tusks dice up feeder goldfish with those choppers (back in the days before I knew the truth about feeder fish), but I've never seen them use those teeth on a like-sized tankmate. In fact, even though the tusk always gets its share of food, it isn't nearly as "in your face" as most wrasses (especially hogfish) are at feeding time.

It is important to purchase only specimens that have been at your local fish store for a few weeks. Tusks are prone to "transport stress," and a few never recover. Once well- acclimated and feeding, however, they are personable "pet" fish that live for years and are tough as nails.

Paddlefin Wrasse

I've selected this fish as perhaps the most durable of a large and varied genus of wrasses, *Thalassoma*. The paddlefin is usually shipped from the Gulf of California (Sea of Cortez), Mexico. It is one of the more uniquely colored of its genus, with a green head and tail, red body, and triangular yellow wedge behind the head. Like the other wrasses we've looked at, it feeds heartily and is generally good with similarly sized tankmates of a boisterous nature. Some individuals are moderately aggressive with other fish but usually not dangerously so; however, like all wrasses, they will make short work of most crustaceans, even cleaner shrimp.

A number of other *Thalassoma* are regularly seen in the trade, especially the bluehead wrasse (*T. bifasciatum*, a Caribbean species) and the lunar wrasse (*T. lunare*, from the Indo-Pacific). Both of these can be excellent aquarium fish, but not always. They are perplexingly inconsistent in hardiness, probably due to point of origin and/or collecting methods used. Bluehead wrasses, in particular, may suffer if they are kept with other blueheads. The blue-headed ones are "supermales" (the females and juveniles are completely yellow). When males are housed together they fight, as you might expect; and even if they are separated, there is a lingering post-traumatic stress from which the fish may not recover. Over the last year or so, most of the blueheads I've seen have been in rough shape, and I currently don't recommend this species.

 PADDLEFIN WRASSE

Thalassoma lucasanum

Geographic Range: Eastern Pacific (especially Gulf of California)

Adult Size: 6 inches (15 cm)

Temperament: moderately aggressive; generally a good tankmate with sturdy species but may intimidate less aggressive species

Food: glass shrimp, krill, brine shrimp, bloodworms, small chunks of all meaty seafoods, and most prepared foods

Sixline Wrasse

Although we have looked at several medium-to-large wrasses, there are also many dwarf species that reach only a few inches. Chief among these are the lined wrasses of the genus *Pseudocheilinus* and the fairy wrasses of the genus *Cirrhilabrus*. We'll take the sixline wrasse as a typical representative of the dwarf wrasses.

 SIXLINE WRASSE

Pseudocheilinus hexataenia

Geographic Range: Indo-Pacific

Adult Size: 3 inches (7.5 cm)

Temperament: moderately aggressive but safe with tankmates that are not too shy

Food: all small meaty items

Pseudocheilinus hexataenia is one of the wrasses generally referred to as "reef safe" in the hobby, meaning that it is not destructive in reef aquariums. In fish-only aquariums they are not really aggressive, but they are feisty. They know what's theirs, and they'll defend it. They may be a bit too much for some of the smaller gobies and generally should not be mixed with the more peaceful fairy wrasses.

Sixline wrasses feed on copepods, other microcrustaceans, and small worms. Reef hobbyists love them because they will eat the bristleworms that are considered pests on live rock. Although somewhat shy at feeding time, they will eat brine shrimp, mysids, bloodworms, blackworms, and perhaps finely chopped pieces of larger foods. They usually have little interest in flakes or pellets, although an occasional specimen will eat them.

JAWFISH

The sixty or so species of the family Opistognathidae are found worldwide in shallow tropical seas. These large-headed fish are living bulldozers, constructing burrows of sand and gravel that they enter tail-first. They are rather goby-like in general appearance but are probably more closely related to basslets. Jawfish sometimes form large colonies, with individuals evenly spaced. They are mouthbrood-

➔ Bali tiger jawfish (Opistognathidae sp.) need a deep, sandy substrate in which to burrow.

ers; the male incubates the eggs. They spawn readily in captivity, but I am not aware of any consistently successful rearing of the young. Although other species appear in the hobby from time to time, our representative, below, will be the one species that is found in every local fish store with a marine section.

Yellowhead Jawfish

This beautiful fish has a yellow head and a white body that is suffused with powder-blue (which inspires the alternate common name of "pearly jawfish"). Believe me when I say, you have to see one in person, as I have never seen a photo that truly does this species justice.

Yellowhead jawfish do best with a deeper substrate (4 to 6 inches [10.2 to 15.2 cm]) to allow them to dig effectively. The substrate should be of varying sizes, including some large pebbles. The jawfish will line the entrances to their burrows with the larger stones and will use them, as would brickmasons, to selectively reinforce the tunnel wall.

 YELLOWHEAD JAWFISH

Opistognathus aurifrons

Geographic Range: Tropical Western Atlantic; Caribbean

Adult Size: 3 inches (7.5 cm)

Temperament: peaceful with other species; territorial with conspecifics but can be kept communally

Food: mysids, krill, brine shrimp, bloodworms, finely chopped seafoods, meat-based flakes and small pellets

For an entertaining display, try setting up a tank of 40 gallons (151 L) or larger with six or more jawfish (or about one for every square foot of substrate). The fish are territorial, but little or no damage is done. Instead, you will see a lot of posturing with gill flaring. It's also very comical to see a jawfish stealing stones when its neighbor's back is turned.

Jawfish settle in quickly and feed on small crustaceans such as brine shrimp, mysids, and small krill.

GOBIES

There are more gobies than any other single family of marine fish. Many estimates put the total number of gobies at more than 2,000 species in some 200 genera! Gobies are found from tropical to subpolar seas, in all oceans (and many species in freshwater, too). There are several families of gobies, but here we will consider species from just two of them: the "typical" gobies of the family Gobiidae and the dart gobies of the family Microdesmidae. Typical gobies have the pelvic fins fused into a suction disk and have a mouth that is terminal (meaning basically straight; neither upturned nor downturned) or subterminal (downturned). Sleeper gobies, such as the dart gobies, do not have completely fused pelvic fins; in fact, in most species they are completely separate. Sleepers also usually have a terminal or supraterminal (upturned) mouth.

With so many species, it is truly hard to generalize about gobies. Almost anything I say will have an exception somewhere in this diverse group. However, the majority of gobies are relatively small, round-headed, cylindrical-bodied benthic fish with two dorsal fins (one soft and one spiny) that are completely separated. The eyes are

➍ Known in the wild for inhabiting muddy waters of estuaries, lagoons, and other coastal waters, the sand goby similarly will burrow into the substrate in your home marine aquarium.

often large and high on the head. They actually look a lot like little aquatic bulldogs (and many act like it, too). Many gobies are small, only 1 or 2 inches (2.5 to 5 cm) in length, although some large sleepers reach about 24 inches (61 cm) in length.

Gobies are what I call "peaceful but territorial." This isn't really as contradictory as it seems. Gobies will stake out a small cave or hole, or, like living bulldozers, make their own by digging into the substrate. Most gobies are homebodies that do not go out looking for trouble but will vigorously drive away intruders, especially intruders of their own species. Their pugnacity is almost purely defensive, and they will live and let live with other species that do not invade their personal space. In my opinion, one advantage of having gobies as part of your fish community is that their bottom-dwelling habits let them occupy a niche that is often vacant in the marine aquarium, whereas many of the species we keep swim in the upper to middle levels of the tank. Another big plus is that most gobies do not need a large aquarium because they are small and are not active swimmers.

Gobies are micropredators that feed primarily on benthic invertebrates (such as worms) and small crustaceans (such as copepods), and in the aquarium they will do well on brine shrimp, bloodworms, krill, and finely chopped pieces of scallop, squid, and other meaty foods. Most species will take flakes and pellets but have little interest in vegetable matter.

Gobies are not delicate and are resistant to most diseases; however, it should be noted that they react poorly to copper-based medications, so alternative treatments should be used if medications are needed. Consult your local fish store.

At least several dozen species of gobies are seen in the hobby with some regularity, and, theoretically, hundreds more are possible from time to time. Obviously, we can only review a select few representatives here.

Blue-Spotted Shrimp Goby

The gobies of the genus *Cryptocentrus* (along with several other genera) are noted for having a fascinating symbiotic relationship with pistol shrimp (genus *Alpheus*). *C. cinctus* is a fairly average shrimp goby that varies from light gray to yellow in color, but has an attractive pattern of polka dots. A single goby, or occasionally a mated pair, will share its burrow with a pistol shrimp. Actually, it might be more correct to say that the shrimp shares its burrow with the goby, because the shrimp is the one that actually excavates and maintains the burrow.

Many researchers define the symbiotic relationship between the goby and the shrimp as commensalism because the goby benefits from having a safe refuge but doesn't give back anything to the shrimp. Others say that it is a mutualistic relationship because the goby has bet-

BLUE-SPOTTED SHRIMP GOBY

Cryptocentrus cinctus

Geographic Range:
Western Pacific

Adult Size: 4 inches
(10 cm)

Temperament: peaceful with other species and generally peaceful with conspecifics

Food: glass shrimp, mysids, krill, brine shrimp, bloodworms, finely chopped seafoods, meat-based flakes and small pellets

ter eyesight than the shrimp and thus serves as a lookout for danger. It's certainly true that when danger threatens, both partners instantly retreat to the depths of the burrow. But, does the goby actually signal some sort of alarm that the shrimp receives? It's hard to say.

Regardless of the details, this symbiotic relationship makes an interesting display that is very different from the standard clownfish-and-anemone symbiosis. It used to be easy to obtain the gobies but difficult to get the shrimp; today, the shrimp are more readily available.

The blue-spotted shrimp goby is a hardy aquarium inhabitant that will eat all live, frozen, and prepared meaty foods. It is not disease prone and is not overly sensitive to changes in water quality. Additionally, it is inexpensive, gets along well with almost all other fish (except, perhaps, another *C. cinctus*, unless there are many hiding places).

Firefish

The firefish is a small sleeper goby that is well-named. It has a yellowish snout and is white on the head and midbody, shading to a deepening orange-red on the hindbody and tail. It has a jaunty, pennant-like first dorsal fin that is raised to indicate fright or aggression but usually carried at about "half mast" when the fish is comfortable. Although *N. magnifica* is the firefish you will usually see at your local fish store, two other species—*N. decora* (purple firefish) and the rare and very expensive *N. helfrichi* (Helfrich's firefish)—are sometimes offered for sale.

Firefish usually are not far from a burrow, but *Nemateleotris* will often hover in midwater, feeding on plankton; they can be combative with each other and, in a small to medium-sized aquarium,

⭐ FIREFISH

Nemateleotris magnifica

Geographic Range: Indo-Pacific

Adult Size: 3.5 inches (8.75 cm)

Temperament: timid with other species; aggressive with conspecifics but can be kept in groups in large tanks

Food: mysids, brine shrimp, bloodworms, and other tiny meat-based foods; sometimes takes flakes or very small pellets

should be kept alone. However, if you have a larger aquarium (about 55 gallons [208 L] or more), firefish will form loose schools. The key seems to be having half a dozen individuals or more, which allows the fish to form a stable pecking order in which all the individuals squabble a little but (usually) no individual gets singled out for all the abuse. When only two or three are kept, one will invariably become the dominant fish and beat up the other(s).

With other species, firefish are peaceful, even shy. They do not do well with extremely boisterous tankmates such as damselfish. They get along better with benthic gobies, small basslets (such as the more peaceful dottybacks like *Pseudochromis fridmani*), small butterfly-fish, and fairy wrasses (*Cirrhilabrus* species).

Firefish should be offered small portions of food at frequent intervals. This will let them feed as they would in nature, where they forage for small plankton from midwater, almost continuously. Ideal foods include mysids, brine shrimp, bloodworms, and finely chopped pieces of larger meaty foods. They may take flake or prepared foods, but probably not eagerly.

Since firefish can be sensitive to water quality variations, strict attention to water quality is required. Variations in pH, high nitrate levels, or other symptoms of poor water quality will stress these fish, causing them to stop eating and possibly fall victim to disease. However, if you are diligent with your maintenance duties, there is no reason to pass on these delightful little fish.

Zebra Goby

The zebra goby is an elongated species with a pale blue body and lovely pink zebra stripes. Its behavior and care in the aquarium are similar in most respects to the firefish. They are usually seen in pairs or in small groups in the wild, and you may be able to create a stable, compatible group in the aquarium if you introduce three or more to your tank at the same time. If you introduce one or two and then later attempt to add more, the established specimens will probably attack the newcomers.

Zebra gobies will also do some burrowing, like their firefish relatives, but in my experience they seem to spend more time in midwater and higher off the bottom than the firefish. Zebra gobies are peaceful with all other fish, hardy in general, and accept all meaty foods.

 ZEBRA GOBY

Ptereleotris zebra

Geographic Range: Indo-Pacific

Adult Size: 4 inches (10 cm)

Temperament: peaceful with other species and conspecifics

Food: mysids, krill, brine shrimp, bloodworms, finely chopped seafoods, meat-based flakes and small pellets

Neon Goby

There are about a half-dozen species of neon gobies, but *Gobiosoma oceanops* is the largest, hardiest, and most readily available at your local fish store. These gobies have black backs and black flanks, and twin neon-blue "racing stripes" that gleam under fluorescent aquarium lights. Other neon goby species have stripes of different colors, often bright gold or white. One especially attractive species is the sharknose neon goby, *G. evelynae*, which often has two-tone neon stripes—gold on the head shading to blue on the body. The other species are smaller, about 1 to 1.5 inches (2.5 to 3.8 cm), but are also good aquarium inhabitants.

Neon gobies are cleaners that pick parasites from the skin and gills of larger fish. They are not unique in this behavior; for example,

NEON GOBY

Gobiosoma oceanops

Geographic Range:
Caribbean

Adult Size: 2 inches
(5 cm)

Temperament: territorial but can be kept in large groups if adequate shelters are available

Food: very tiny foods, such as brine shrimp, bloodworms, and mysids; flake foods and tiny pellets

the cleaner wrasses (the Indo-Pacific genus *Labroides*), juveniles of many butterflyfish and angelfish species, and numerous shrimp species also provide this service. However, neon gobies are perhaps the most conspicuous cleaners on Caribbean coral reefs. The gobies set up cleaning stations where their bright stripes apparently advertise their service, and "customers" may actually wait in line. It is startling to see the neon gobies working their way deep into the gaping mouths of large groupers or moray eels and emerging unharmed.

Neon gobies are extremely peaceful with other fish species, and are too small to harass invertebrates. They will squabble among themselves, but not severely, and large groups can be kept together if there are enough hiding places (such as empty snail shells) to allow each goby to have a home of its own.

Some cleaner fish, specifically the cleaner wrasses, feed only on fish parasites and are almost impossible to keep alive in the aquarium. Fortunately, neon gobies aren't like that. They are good cleaners but don't depend on parasites (which hopefully your fish have few or none of!) for sustenance. They also feed on benthic invertebrates, and in the aquarium they will accept all meaty foods of appropriate size.

Neon gobies are captive bred in large numbers for the aquarium trade, and most of those you see in your local fish store do not come from the wild. In fact, if you keep a group, you will almost certainly have them spawning at some point. They lay eggs in a sheltered crevice (part of the reason they do so well in small snail shells), which the male then guards until the planktonic larvae emerge. This is the hard part. The gobies are easy to spawn, but not easy to raise unless you make the commitment to raise rotifers (small, multicellular plankton such as *Brachionus* species). I applaud you if you want to give it a try, but the details are outside the focus of this book.

Citron Goby

The stout little coral gobies of the genus *Gobiodon*, with about a dozen species, are favorites of aquarists. These fish have large heads (even for gobies) and bodies that are flattened but very deep; that is, they are tall from top to bottom but short from front to back. They have toxic slime that deters all predators, but they (unlike the soapfish) are too small for this defense to pose a risk of poisoning an entire aquarium.

The citron goby, *G. citrinus*, is probably the most popular species. It's easy to see why: With its lemon-yellow body and thin white stripes on the head and along the base of the dorsal fins, it is very attractive. It is sometimes confused with the related yellow coral goby, *G. okinawae*. However, the two species are easy to distinguish: the yellow coral goby is smaller (about 1.5 inches [3.8 cm]) and lacks the contrasting white stripes of the citron goby.

 CITRON GOBY

Gobiodon citrinus

Geographic Range: Indo-Pacific

Adult Size: 2.5 inches (6.25 cm)

Temperament: peaceful; often forms mated pairs in the aquarium

Food: very tiny foods, such as brine shrimp, bloodworms, and mysids; may take flake foods and tiny pellets

Because they don't bother any invertebrates, except for small copepods and worms, *G. citrinus* and its relatives are favored by those who keep reef tanks. But, there is no reason they shouldn't be considered for an aquarium consisting of small, friendly fish. They will usually fight with each other, but sometimes a stable mated pair will form. In the wild, coral gobies are usually found in association with large plate corals (*Acropora*), and they will appreciate it if you duplicate this with the appropriate coral replicas in their aquarium. They will thrive on mysids, brine shrimp, small krill, and bloodworms.

SURGEONFISH

Surgeonfish or tangs (family Acanthuridae) are another group of fish that are conspicuous fixtures on coral reefs. The more than seventy species are circumtropical in distribution; the majority are found in

The pointy spines along the base of the tail fin are a noticeable characteristic of most surgeonfish such as this clown tang (also called a striped surgeonfish).

the Indo-Pacific. Most species are disc-shaped or oval with large eyes, small mouths, and tiny scales.

The characteristic feature of the family is a set of defensive spines in the caudal peduncle. In most species, these razor-sharp spines are retractable and are flicked out like switchblades to slash an attacker with a slap of the tail. In a few species (genus *Naso*) the spines are fixed but still hazardous.

Tangs are often social in the wild, and it may be possible to keep them in schools if you have plenty of space for these active, midwater fish. Mixed-species schools of surgeonfish make a particularly nice display. Just be sure to introduce them all at the same time and make sure that no individual is significantly larger than the rest. With other fish, they are placid, with the exception of a very few aggressive species. However, they will not back down from a confrontation yet seem surprisingly reluctant to use their "switchblades" on a tankmate unless sorely provoked.

Most surgeonfish graze on macroalgae or microalgae, and they are almost certain to develop HLLE if they do not get a balanced diet. Of the several dozen surgeonfish species that occur with some regularity in the trade, I've picked four especially good subjects for the beginning marine aquarist.

Hippo Tang

This is the blue companion of the clownfish in *Finding Nemo*. Thanks to the movie, the popularity of hippo tangs soared, and they now cost about triple what they did before! Be cautious when selecting one to ensure that it has a full appearance and is not "pinched" behind the head (concave temples). Stressed, skinny fish rarely recover. These fish often associate with *Acropora* corals when

HIPPO TANG

Paracanthurus hepatus

Geographic Range: Indo-Pacific

Adult Size: 10 inches (25 cm)

Temperament: peaceful with other species; usually peaceful with conspecifics, especially when young

Food: nori, blanched peas, and other greens; tang-specific frozen foods; younger fish consume more protein (brine shrimp, mysids)

young. Frightened fish will dive deep into a coral head and become almost impossible to remove.

This tang has pluses and minuses as an aquarium fish. When healthy upon arrival, not stressed by aggressive tankmates, and fed a varied diet, it is a tough and long-lived species that is easily kept with conspecifics and all other species. However, if water quality is not absolutely optimum, and if they do not receive lots of veggies and supplementation of vitamins A and C in particular, this is probably the most likely tang to develop HLLE.

Sailfin Tang

The surgeonfish of the genus *Zebrasoma* are collectively known as sailfin tangs, but *Z. desjardinii* is the most "sailfinny" of them all!

 SAILFIN TANG

Zebrasoma desjardinii

Geographic Range: Indo-Pacific

Adult Size: 14 inches (35 cm)

Temperament: peaceful with other species and usually with conspecifics

Food: nori and all other vegetable based foods, tang-specific frozen foods

Adults have an intricate pattern of stripes on their bodies and spots on their fins (although there is some overlap) and have exceptionally tall dorsal fins and deep anal fins. Although it is a large species that needs a tank of 125 gallons (473 L) or larger when mature, the sailfin tang is a showy fish that is also hardy and accepts a wide range of aquarium foods. However, as with all tangs, its diet should contain more vegetable matter than anything else. It is peaceful with all tankmates, even with conspecifics (for the most part).

I should note that some ichthyologists recognize two species of sailfin tangs, based on some differences in color pattern: *Z. desjardinii* from the Indian Ocean and *Z. veliferum* from the Pacific Ocean.

Yellow Tang

The yellow tang is near the top of the list of marine fish you will find in practically every local fish store. It is geographically widespread, but there is general agreement that the prettiest and hardiest specimens come from Hawaii. Yellow tangs are gregarious and look best and behave more naturally in large groups. There is always the chance of a smaller or weaker individual being bullied in such an arrangement, but it is rare. Other fish will not be disturbed.

Yellow tangs are among the sturdiest in terms of overall hardiness and disease resistance, but they do sometimes display an annoying susceptibility to black spot disease, which is not ich, as some have claimed, but is a parasitic flatworm. Unless a tang is really loaded with these parasites, quarantine and regular freshwater dips usually serve to eradicate the infestation.

 YELLOW TANG

Zebrasoma flavescens

Geographic Range: Indo-Pacific

Adult Size: 8 inches (20 cm)

Temperament: peaceful with other species, gregarious with conspecifics

Food: nori and all other vegetable based foods; tang-specific frozen foods; also needs krill and brine shrimp to maintain bright color

Yellow tangs are very prone to color loss and need lots of greens in their diet, along with krill and brine shrimp, to help prevent this. There are also some newer frozen prepared foods that are formulated especially for tangs, and these are getting positive buzz from tang fans.

Purple Tang

Like many other Red Sea fish, the purple tang was once a rarity that carried an exorbitant price tag, if you were lucky enough to find one. Recent years have seen more reliable supplies of many Red Sea fish, and the prices of some species have dropped considerably. The purple tang is now easily available and, although it isn't as cheap as a yellow tang, won't break the bank. That's a good thing, as this is the best *Zebrasoma* for the aquarium. It is a rugged fish that adapts effortlessly to aquarium life. Additionally, it is gentle with non-tang tankmates, good with conspecifics, and holds its color better than a number of other tang species. The purple tang slightly eclipses the yellow tang in positive attributes, and I would give it the nod as your first try with a tang.

 PURPLE TANG

Zebrasoma xanthurum

Geographic Range: Red Sea

Adult Size: 9 inches (22.5 cm)

Temperament: peaceful with other species and generally peaceful with conspecifics

Food: nori and all other greens; tang-specific frozen foods

TRIGGERFISH

Triggerfish (family Balistidae) are sometimes called "leatherjackets" because of their thick, tough skin. There are only about forty species, but they are found in all tropical oceans. The fused pelvic fins form a spine. Additionally, the first dorsal spine has a triggerlike locking mechanism—a second spine that locks into place and prevents the heavy first spine from being depressed. When alarmed, a triggerfish will swim into a tight crevice, wedge the first spine tight into the coral, and activate the trigger mechanism. The fish is then almost

impossible for a predator to remove. The jaws are beaklike, with large and powerful teeth. Most triggerfish are solitary, day-active carnivores that wander slowly over sand flats, blowing jets of water to expose crabs or urchins, which they then dismember with their teeth. Triggers are especially adept at blowing urchins over to attack them at their short-spined undersides.

Triggerfish normally swim with undulating movements of the soft second dorsal and anal fins, but will use the tail for emergency bursts. In the aquarium, there usually is not much that constitutes an emergency. Triggers are large, strong fish, and many species are frighteningly aggressive. However, I acknowledge that there is always a market for mean fish, and I won't say there's anything wrong with that if that's what floats your boat!

Blue-and-Gold Triggerfish

The blue-and-gold triggerfish is probably the winner of the Most Aggressive Trigger award. It's big and quite beautiful, but seems almost psychotic toward tankmates. It is definitely a fish that needs to be kept alone; but, like the other big triggers, you probably couldn't kill one with a stick!

A notable tendency of triggers is that they are hard on equipment. They like to bite filter tubes, crunch powerheads, shatter heaters, etc. Obviously, when they damage something electrical, they stand a good chance of electrocuting themselves in the process. Your local fish store will probably sell specially constructed plastic shields for heaters, but you may need to improvise to protect other devices.

BLUE-AND-GOLD TRIGGERFISH

Balistapus undulatus

Geographic Range:
Western Pacific; Indian Ocean

Adult Size: 14 inches (35 cm)

Temperament:
Extremely aggressive; probably must be kept alone

Food: anything meaty

Clown Triggerfish

The battleship of the triggerfish clan—this big, colorful, but ultimately nasty fish certainly has its fans. When young (up to 6 or 8 inches [15.2 to 20.3 cm] in length), it is possible to keep a clown trigger with groupers, large volitans lionfish, and other fish that are aggressive, toothy, or venomous. When it gets some real size, however, the clown trigger's aggression tends to increase, too. When it is an adult you will find that you need to devote a large tank to a single fish. Some people don't have a problem with that, but, if you do, it would be best to avoid this species.

 CLOWN TRIGGERFISH

Balistoides conspicillum

Geographic Range:
Western Pacific; Indian Ocean

Adult Size: 18 inches (50 cm)

Temperament: very aggressive; ferocity increases with size

Food: anything meaty

Clowns, like many large triggers, seem to have their own sense of aesthetics, and delight in rearranging the decor. You can try to create an attractive aquascape in a trigger tank, but don't be surprised if the trigger constantly moves rockwork and coral. By the way, beware when working in a trigger's tank. They are not afraid to use their powerful jaws and big teeth on you!

On the positive side, clown triggers are known to live for twenty years or more in captivity. They almost never succumb to any disease, and they will eat anything meaty. Try not to overfeed them, though, as they easily become overweight.

Niger Triggerfish

With its blue-green colors and long tail filaments, the Niger trigger is a highly decorative species. Fortunately, it is also only moderately aggressive. It can't be kept with conspecifics, but it will not be a killer in a tank of large wrasses, big angels such as *Holacanthus* species, and other tough customers. However, take care not to keep it with

 NIGER TRIGGERFISH

Odonus niger

Geographic Range: Indo-Pacific

Adult Size: 18 inches (50 cm)

Temperament: moderately aggressive; can be kept with other species but not with conspecifics

Food: all meaty foods

species that would nip at its tail filaments, such as puffers and some large wrasses. Many other triggerfish are somewhat slow-moving except when on the attack, and may hang close to the bottom or near a cave or crevice. The Niger trigger, however, is quite active and will cruise regally in midwater at a good pace. Thus, even a small specimen should be kept in a roomy tank (at least 55 gallons [208 L]), and moved to proportionately larger tanks as it grows. The Niger trigger is also known as the "red-toothed triggerfish" because it displays crimson teeth; these are most obvious in full-grown individuals.

PICASSO TRIGGERFISH

Rhinecanthus aculeatus

Geographic Range: Indo-Pacific

Adult Size: 10 inches (25 cm)

Temperament: peaceful to moderately aggressive; can be kept with other species but not with conspecifics

Food: anything meaty

Picasso Triggerfish

This is the famed humuhumu nukunuku apua'a, the state fish of Hawaii. If you are interested in triggers but don't want to deal with the over-the-top aggression of the larger species, then *Rhinecanthus* are for you, and *R. aculeatus* is the most available species. A Picasso trigger shouldn't be kept with small fish or with nervous butterfly-fish, or the like; but with sturdy fish of similar size, it is almost peaceful. It will eat anything small enough to swallow and will dice most larger foods until they are.

CHAPTER 5

Keeping Fish Healthy

Fish aren't like us. Humans and other mammals are very expressive, especially with our facial features and body language, and one of the things we express well is when we are feeling ill. Fish lack expressive facial features and have a very different sort of body language; if you train yourself to look at some key parts of a fish's body, you can unlock this language and make some pretty good assessments of a fish's health.

SIGNS OF ILLNESS

The old adage says that "the eyes have it," and, indeed, you can tell a lot by looking at a fish's eyes. They should be clear, not cloudy or opaque, and they should be full and well-rounded, not flat or sunken. They should be responsive; that is, it should be fairly obvious whether a fish can see normally. Many fish will look right at you. If you see a fish picking at food and navigating around the tank without bumping into things, it's a good indication that the fish has normal vision. Conversely, cloudy eyes and uncoordinated behavior may indicate stress and/or disease. Look also at the skin behind the eyes (roughly what you might call the "temples," I guess). This area should not have a pinched or sunken look.

Fins are also a good indication of a fish's mood and stress level. Fins should be whole, not split, tattered, or with red or white edges. Healthy fish often carry the fins erect. Especially important are the pelvic fins, usually located in the chest region, and the pectoral fins, which are usually immediately behind the gill covers. A healthy fish uses these paired fins to maneuver, and you will see many species paddling with the pectoral fins and flicking the pelvic fins to steer. An unhealthy fish, however, often clamps all of its fins tight to the body and even folds the tail. Clamped fins are often accompanied by shimmying.

The fish's skin should be free of cysts, blemishes, inflamed red areas, or thick mucus that sloughs off in patches. Any of these could indicate a bacterial or parasitic infection. Another telltale sign of these problems is scratching behavior; a fish approaches the gravel or a decoration and makes a rapid, glancing contact with it. Look also at the mouth and the skin around it; if the mouth appears to be paralyzed in a half-open position, or if the skin around it is inflamed (especially in small-mouthed species such as angelfish, butterflyfish, and tangs), the fish usually won't recover.

Rapid breathing is another sign of illness. It may be hard for you to recognize this at first. Like us, fish will normally breathe more rapidly when exerting themselves, such as when they chase food. Rapid breathing that is abnormal is also very shallow, and is usually combined with one or more of the other symptoms above. For example, a sick fish may shimmy in place, with clamped fins and rapid breathing. If you learn to read the body language of fish, you should have no trouble selecting healthy specimens. But selecting a healthy fish is only part of your challenge, Grasshopper!

SETTING UP A QUARANTINE TANK

In many cases it is very difficult to treat a disease outbreak in a display aquarium. This is especially true if the tank contains any invertebrates, because the levels of common fish medications (such as copper sulfate) necessary to treat a parasitic problem, such as an ich outbreak, will wipe out all the "inverts." Medications are not without risks to the fish, either. In many cases there is a fine line between the level of a medication that will kill the parasites and the level that will kill the fish!

For these reasons, among others, I strongly recommend the use of a quarantine tank for any newly purchased fish. This lets you isolate a new specimen from your main fish community and observe it under controlled conditions to see if problems develop. If your new acquisition does develop some disease, it can be treated safely.

A quarantine tank should be as simple as possible. I prefer a 10- or 20-gallon (38- or 75-L) tank with a large sponge filter (fully cycled with nitrifying bacteria), a very thin layer of substrate, and one good hiding place (a rock, an artificial coral, or even a more clinical shelter such as a piece of PVC pipe).

Some folks use medications such as copper preventively in the quarantine tank or will administer short freshwater dips to reduce or eliminate parasites. These approaches are valid but can increase anxiety in an already stressed fish. I prefer to use the quarantine tank as a safe haven in which a new fish can settle in slowly and without disturbance. I simply observe the new acquisition for a minimum of two weeks; if all is well, I then transfer the fish to the display tank.

> ### SIGNS OF A HEALTHY FISH
>
> **Eyes:** clear (not cloudy), bright, responsive (move and follow objects)
> **Fins:** clear and free of blemishes, spots, lesions (note: be careful not to mistake normal coloration for disease–related spots)
> **Skin:** free of cysts, blemishes, inflamed red areas, or thick mucus that sloughs off in patches
> **Mouth:** not inflamed and/or frozen open
> **Head:** should not have a "pinched" appearance (concave, sunken skin) behind the eyes
> **Swimming pattern:** active; beware of listless, slow, unresponsive movement or scratching behavior
> **Breathing:** not rapid and/or shallow

It is not a flawless procedure, but I believe that if you religiously quarantine new arrivals, you will have few, if any, disease problems in your main tank.

AILMENTS AND TREATMENTS

Sooner or later you will be confronted with a disease or parasite problem. I hope that by employing strict quarantine of all new arrivals we can keep your problems to a minimum, or at least keep them away from your display tank and main community of fish.

We don't have the space here for a thorough review of all the diseases that could be encountered by the marine aquarist. There are hundreds, maybe thousands. I can, however, give you an introduction to several of the most common illnesses you may encounter, as well as offer you some tips on treating them.

Parasitic problems are undoubtedly the number one disease headache of marine aquarists. Almost all wild-caught marine fish carry some parasites externally or internally. In the wild, most parasites are unlikely to be more than a minor irritant because they rarely build up to life-threatening numbers on an individual fish. When a parasite reproduces, its progeny disperse and probably do not re-infest the same fish. In an aquarium, however, there's nowhere to run, and the multiplication of a parasite can crash a whole tank's population of fish if left unchecked.

Saltwater Ich

Protozoans are the most common parasites in the marine aquarium, and the most frequent is saltwater ich. Like the freshwater variety, this usually manifests as small (about 1 mm), whitish cysts on the skin and gills of an affected fish. Affected fish usually clamp their fins, breathe rapidly (due to parasites on the gills interfering with breathing), and stop eating. There are at least two different protozoans that are lumped under the heading of ich: *Cryptocaryon irritans* and *Amyloodinium ocellatum*. (The latter has smaller cysts and is sometimes known as "saltwater velvet.") The cysts grow and eventually fall off the fish, then the cyst breaks open to release swarmers that infest new fish (or re-infest the same one). The swarmer stage is when the fish are vulnerable.

The standard treatment for both types of ich is a copper sulfate solution, many brands of which are available at your local fish store. If an outbreak occurs in your display tank, you will have to treat the whole tank. But, if you have any invertebrates, they must be removed and can never return. Once a tank is treated with copper, a trace level will always be present—not enough to harm fish, but enough to kill almost all invertebrates. You will also need a copper test kit to monitor copper levels, because the copper binds to the calcium carbonate in your substrate and is rendered inactive; thus, you have to keep adding copper, perhaps daily, to maintain an effective ich-killing level. The effective level is about two parts per million, which is several times less than the level that is lethal to most fish (although scaleless fish and tiny fish, such as some gobies, are sensitive to even low levels of copper). The copper level should be

⊕ This Helfrich's firefish is plagued by saltwater ich, an parasitic disorder that manifests as whitish cysts on the skin and gills.

maintained for three to four weeks, even if all visible cysts disappear much sooner, because ich has an annoying tendency to bounce back if treatment is discontinued too soon.

Flukes

Parasitic flatworms such as *Brooklynella* are often present on the gills and/or skin of wild-caught fish. These nasties are among the parasites that cleaner shrimp and a number of small fish specialize in removing from large fish. Some fish groups are notoriously susceptible to gill flukes, so much so that fluke infestations are often called "angelfish disease" or "clownfish disease."

Treatment involves periodic dips into a bucket of tank water that has been treated with a 37 percent formalin 3 solution. This is available from your local fish store. Follow the directions carefully and do not exceed the recommended dose. Formalin removes oxygen from the water, so the dip bucket must be vigorously aerated with an airstone. An infested fish is placed in the dip for forty to forty-five minutes, every other day. Three to four treatments are usually sufficient to eradicate the flukes. Never use formalin on a display tank, as it will wipe out your nitrifying bacteria and every invertebrate.

Lymphocystis

Now we come to a disease that is unsightly but not fatal. Lymphocystis is a viral infection that causes large, cauliflower-like lumps to grow on the fins and heads of affected fish. It does not appear to be very contagious; in many cases a single fish in a tank will be badly affected while all the others remain clear. In its early stages it can be mistaken for *Cryptocaryon*, so, if you see a case of

◑ This queen angelfish has a nasty case of lymphocystis. Though this untreatable viral disease rarely ends in mortality, the lesions may leave an infected fish awfully disfigured.

ich that does not respond to copper, it may be early lymphocystis. There is no treatment; with time, however, the lesions usually fade and eventually disappear.

Head-and-Lateral-Line Erosion

This tongue-twister condition, usually abbreviated HLLE, is a bit of a mystery. The symptoms are loss of pigment and inflammation on the head and along the lateral line (the fluid-filled canals along the flank

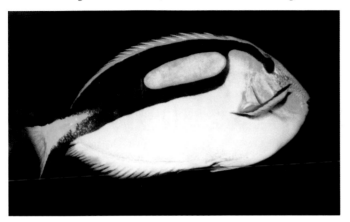

◒ This hippo tang's loss of pigmentation is evidence of head-and-lateral line erosion, a disease that most commonly afflicts surgeonfish and probably is caused by nutritional deficiencies.

of a fish that sense water pressure changes). The condition does not appear to be fatal, but a fish that is badly afflicted can become rather hideous.

The jury is still out on the exact cause, but there does not appear to be any pathogen involved; at least, no one has been able to isolate one. The common denominator is probably a dietary deficiency. One clue is that the two groups of fish that are most commonly afflicted with HLLE are tangs and angelfish, both being groups in which most species are heavily vegetarian. Prevention and reversal of HLLE should include large amounts of varied vegetable matter in the diet and regular soaking of food items in a vitamin/mineral supplement (especially vitamins A and C) before feeding. Additionally, high nitrate levels are believed by some to play a role, so it would not hurt to do large water changes regularly and perhaps even use one of the commercial "nitrate sponge" products.

Conclusion

SOME PARTING WORDS

We've reached the end of the line for this first journey into the marvelous world of marine aquariums. From this point on, attentive and regular maintenance is the key to success. To summarize a bit: Replace water lost to evaporation, but also replace a minimum of 15 percent of the water with freshly mixed seawater at least monthly. Scrape algae as necessary, clean and replace filter media at least several times per year and monitor ammonium, nitrite, nitrate, and pH at least weekly. Periodically check for phosphate buildup. Scrub off any salt creep that dries around the edges of your tank lid or filters. Feed your fish as wide a variety of foods as they will accept, but not too much. Give your fish plenty of room to swim, hide, and grow; and constantly observe their social interactions. Most of all, sit back and enjoy your aquarium!

ABOUT THE AUTHOR

Ray Hunziker has been keeping aquariums for more than thirty-five years. A marine biology graduate of the University of North Carolina at Wilmington, he was a longtime editor of *Tropical Fish Hobbyist* magazine and has authored or coauthored more than ten books and dozens of articles on fish, reptiles, amphibians, invertebrates, and other subjects. He lives in Cleveland, Ohio, with a menagerie of fishes and other creatures.

Resources

WEB SITES

Marine Aquarium Council

http://www.aquariumcouncil.org
MAC is an international, not-for-profit organization that brings marine aquarium animal collectors, exporters, importers, and retailers together with aquarium keepers, public aquariums, conservation organizations, and government agencies to conserve coral reefs and other marine ecosystems by creating standards and certification for those engaged in the collection and care of ornamental marine life from reef to aquarium.

American Zoo and Aquarium Association

http://www.aza.org
This nonprofit organization (which was founded in 1924 as the American Association of Zoological Parks and Aquariums) provides information on its Web site about public aquariums nationwide.

LiveAquaria.org

http://www.liveaquaria.org
Owned and operated by Drs. Foster and Smith, renowned as the nation's leading pet product experts, this is a well-regarded online source for marine fish and invertebrates and supplies.

Marine Aquarium Advice

http://www.marineaquariumadvice.com
Here you'll find discussion forums and live chats for beginners to advanced aquarists covering: setting up your first tank, lighting, aquarium photography, disease treatments, do-it-yourself projects, equipment, water chemistry, and other aspects of marine aquariums.

Reef Central

http://www.reefcentral.com
Visit this online community for information about the marine and reef aquarium hobby for all levels of hobbyists.

WetWebMedia

http://www.wetwebmedia.com
This is an excellent site for husbandry information on many species of marine fish and marine aquarium setup and maintenance.

FishBase

http://www.fishbase.org
FishBase is a research tool for nomenclature and scientific information on fish species, genera, and families.

FURTHER READING

Burgess, W.E., H.R. Axelrod, and R.E. Hunziker III. *Dr. Burgess' Mini Atlas of Marine Aquarium Fishes*, 2nd edition. Neptune, N.J.: T.F.H. Publications, Inc., 1997.

Fautin, D.G., and G.R. Allen. *Anemone Fishes and Their Host Sea Anemones*. Melle, Germany: Tetra-Press, 1994.

Fenner, R.M. *The Conscientious Marine Aquarist: A Commonsense Handbook for Successful Saltwater Hobbyists*. Neptune, N.J.: T.F.H. Publications, Inc., 1998.

Michael, S.W. *Angelfishes & Butterflyfishes: Plus Ten More Aquarium Fish Families With Expert Captive Care Advice for the Marine Aquarist*. Neptune, N.J., and Shelburne, Vt.: T.F.H. Publications, Inc., Microcosm Ltd., 2004.

———. *Basslets, Dottybacks & Hawkfishes: Plus Seven More Aquarium Fish Families with Expert Captive Care Advice for the Marine Aquarist*. Neptune, N.J., and Shelburne, VT: T.F.H. Publications, Inc., Microcosm Ltd., 2004.

———. *Reef Fishes*. Vol. 1. Shelburne, Vt.: Microcosm Ltd., 1998.

Randall, J.E. *Caribbean Reef Fishes*, 3rd ed. Neptune, N.J.: T.F.H. Publications, Inc., 1996.

Glossary

Acidic A solution having an excess of hydrogen ions.

Aerobic Processes that require oxygen (for example, the nitrogen cycle).

Alkaline A solution having a low level of hydrogen ions.

Alkalinity The ability of a solution to resist acidification.

Airstone A porous "stone" of wood, silica, or plastic that produces fine bubbles when air is forced through it by an air pump.

Anaerobic Processes functioning in the absence of oxygen (for example, decay).

Aquascaping Collective term for aquarium decorations and their artful arrangement.

Benthic Bottom-dwelling.

Bio-balls Perforated plastic spheres used as a biological filter medium, especially in trickle filters.

Biological filtration Using colonies of aerobic (nitrifying) bacteria to break down nitrogenous wastes (*See also* nitrogen cycle).

Buffering The ability of a solution to resist a change in pH.

Calcareous Containing calcium carbonate ($CaCO_3$).

Canister filter Large, freestanding power filter with a motor sitting atop a large container that is usually compartmentalized for various filter media.

Caudal peduncle Base of a fish's tail.

Ceramic "noodles" Small, noodle-shaped biological filter medium with a high surface area for bacterial colonization.

Chemical filtration Nonbiological removal (for example, using activated carbon) of potentially harmful chemicals.

Chiller Small refrigeration unit for lowering the temperature of aquarium water.

Cirri Hairlike structures on the heads of some fishes.

Conspecific A member of the same species.

Crash (a tank crash) Complete failure of an aquarium system and the deaths of most or all inhabitants.

Dissociation The breaking of a chemical compound, especially a salt, into two or more charged ions.

Dither fish A fast-moving midwater fish intended to draw shy fish out of hiding or serve as a diversion for the aggression of pugnacious fish.

Dorsal fin Fin(s) running along the top (backbone) side of a fish.

Gill cover Large, movable bony flap, often in two or more parts, that protects the gill of a fish and moves in and out as a fish breathes.

Gill flukes Parasitic flatworms that may infest the gills of wild-caught fish and can be transferred to tankmates of a fish that has not been properly quarantined.

Gut-loaded Refers to food animals that have gastrointestinal tracts deliberately loaded with nutritious food and/or vitamin supplements.

Heater Thermostatically controlled unit for maintaining a preset stable aquarium temperature.

Hermaphrodite Animal that can function reproductively as either male or female, but usually not self-fertilizing.

HLLE Head-and-lateral-line erosion, a degenerative dietary deficiency disease of some marine fish.

Hydrometer A device for measuring specific gravity.

Hydrophilic Attracted to water.

Hydrophobic Repelled by water.

Ion Atom with an electrical charge; for example, when dissolved in water, the salt sodium chloride (NaCl) breaks (dissociates) into sodium (Na^+ and chlorine (Cl^-) ions.

Live rock Harvested or aquacultured rock—laden with nitrifying bacteria, plants, and other marine organisms—which is used as both decoration and filtration in marine aquariums.

Live sand Wet aragonite (a calcareous mineral) that contains thriving colonies of aerobic bacteria.

Mechanical filtration Use of pads and flosses to remove large particles from the water.

Molariform Molar-like (teeth).

Mouthbrooder Fish that incubates its eggs in the mouth (for example, jawfish and cardinalfish).

Nitrifying bacteria Aerobic bacteria that drive the nitrogen cycle.

Nitrogen cycle The breakdown of nitrogenous fish wastes into less toxic chemicals (ammonium to nitrite to nitrate) through the action of beneficial bacteria.

Ocellus False eye spot usually intended to confuse predators.

Operculum *See* gill cover.

pH Measurement of the level of hydrogen ions in a solution on a scale from 1 (acidic) to 14 (alkaline or basic).

Power filter A plastic box filter using a magnetically driven impeller to pump water into the filter box, where it is passed through filter media.

Powerhead Small submersible water pump often used to drive an under-gravel filter.

Preopercule Forward gill cover.

Protein skimmer A cylindrical column that draws water from the tank and swirls it around with extremely fine bubbles; the bubbles remove proteins and other large molecules and concentrate them in a collection cup.

Salinity Total dissolved salts in seawater, usually around 35 parts per thousand.

Salt creep Salt crust around tank covers, filter lids, and other devices formed by drying salt spray.

Saltwater Literally, water that contains salt; not synonymous with seawater.

Seawater Natural or artificially produced ocean water that contains salts and numerous trace elements.

Silica sand A substrate type with a high silicon content; similar to if not synonymous with sandbox play sand.

Specific gravity The measure of the density of a water sample compared with pure (distilled) water.

Sponge filter Filter constructed of polyurethane foam that has a tremendous amount of surface area for nitrifying bacteria to colonize.

Subterminal (mouth) Downward-facing mouth opening; usually a characteristic of a bottom-feeding fish.

Sump Water reservoir, especially in a trickle filter.

Supraterminal (mouth) Upward-facing mouth opening; usually a characteristic of a top-feeding fish.

Supraorbital Above the eye.

Symbiosis Partnership between two organisms; may take the form of mutualism, commensalism, or parasitism.

Terminal (mouth) Mouth opening that is neither upward- or downward-facing; generally a characteristic of a fish that feeds at any level.

Top predator Predator that has few to no predators of its own.

Trace elements Elements found in vanishingly small quantities in natural seawater, in theory, practically every known chemical element should be detectable in seawater if the testing is sensitive enough.

Trickle filters A large filter box that is placed under the aquarium; water enters a reservoir or sump on one side of the filter, where a submersible motor pumps a spray of water over plastic "bio-balls" that serve as the medium on which nitrifying bacteria grow.

Ultraviolet sterilizer An opaque cylinder containing a tube that emits ultraviolet radiation to kill free-floating viruses, bacteria, and parasites; usually an add-on to filters.

Undergravel filter Perforated plastic plate that covers the entire bottom of an aquarium and is buried under the gravel, with cylindrical lift tubes in the rear corners.

Index